Travels with my cello

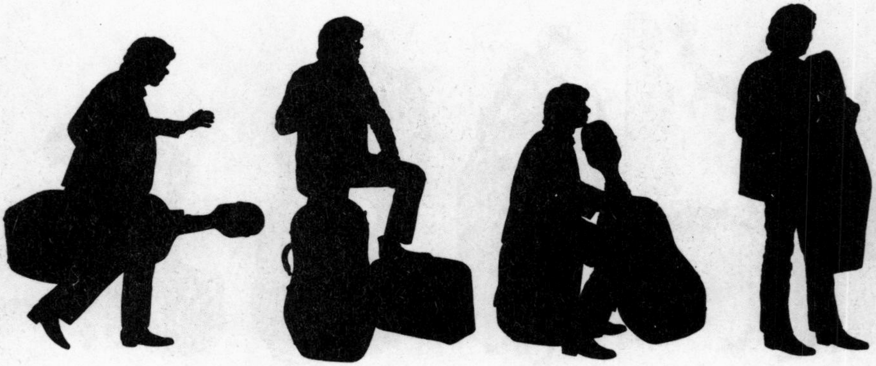

JULIAN LLOYD WEBBER

Travels with my cello

PAVILION
MICHAEL JOSEPH

ACKNOWLEDGEMENT

I would like to thank my wife Celia whose untiring help and support has made so many of the events in this book possible and who plays the typewriter so beautifully.

First published in Great Britain in 1984
by Pavilion Books Limited
196 Shaftesbury Avenue, London WC2H 8JL
in association with Michael Joseph Limited
44 Bedford Square, London WC1B 3DU

Copyright © 1984 Julian Lloyd Webber

Designed by Lawrence Edwards

ISBN 0 907516 27 0

Typeset by Cambrian Typesetters, Aldershot, Hants
Printed in Great Britain by Hollen Street Press Limited, Slough
and bound by Hunter & Foulis Limited, Edinburgh

TO MY MOTHER

Life at Harrington Court — the large, run-down, late Victorian, red brick block of flats just by South Kensington tube — was chiefly memorable for the astonishing, ear-blowing volume of musical decibels which seemed to burst forth from every room most of the day and night. My father's electric organ, mother's piano, grandmother's deafening (she was deaf) television, elder brother's astounding piano and French Horn and my own scrapings on the cello and blowings on the trumpet by themselves would have made the cannon and mortar effects of the *1812 Overture* seem a bit like the aural equivalent of a wet Sunday morning on Hackney Marshes, but when concert-pianist John Lill and record-fiend Tim Rice moved in as well, it was a wonder and a tribute to the sturdy qualities of turn-of-the-century British builders that the whole block of flats didn't descend on to the Piccadilly line below.

We were all on the top floor, so luckily there was no-one to be disturbed above, but below us lived actor Carleton Hobbs. However many tributes he may have received for his radio performances as Sherlock Holmes, nothing can match his award as the world's most long-suffering neighbour. I can recall only two occasions in twenty bone-jarring years on which he complained — the first when for some reason I emptied a bag of bricks on the floor, and then

1

when brother Andrew's stamping on his loud pedal and right heel finally proved too much for Mr Carleton Hobbs's ceiling.

It was hardly surprising with all this going on around and about me that I should have developed an early interest in music. My mother specialised in teaching the piano to young children and was very successful at it — except with me. I was sat in front of a piano when I was four but from the beginning hated every minute of it. Somehow I could never get both hands working together properly at the same time, which proved a slight disadvantage. Then I remember being taken to one of those Ernest Read children's concerts at the Royal Festival Hall. They played the *Sorcerer's Apprentice* and I was riveted by the cellos in the orchestra. Perhaps it was the sight rather than the sound which fascinated me.

I've always thought the cello is a very physical instrument — and by that I don't just mean that it vaguely approximates the shape of a woman. You can see exactly what the player is doing and exactly how the notes are produced and the sound is made — it seemed to me to be a very natural-looking instrument for a human being to play. Anyway lurking in the back, or more likely pretty near the front, of my mind was the wonderful idea that if I started playing another instrument I could probably, with a bit of subtle manoeuvring, give up the dreaded piano.

So I persuaded my parents to buy me a cello.

What arrived was not, much to my disappointment, one of those magnificent-looking things I had seen that day at the Festival Hall but what, I was told, was definitely the right sort of thing for a boy of five to learn on. It was, I later discovered, a *10th*-sized cello — not really much bigger than a big violin — so it was a distinctly disgruntled little boy who sat down to draw his first notes with the bow. But it was good, I liked it, and spent a lot of time playing with my new toy while making quite sure there was no time left to go near the piano.

I began having lessons with a lovely old lady called

2

Alison Dalrymple who had quite a reputation for starting people off on the cello. I remember one of her older pupils at the time was a girl called Jacqueline du Pré.

There is obviously no truth in my mother's account of these lessons:

'Parents used to be encouraged to stay during the lessons and, as they were mostly musicians themselves, to accompany their offspring on the piano. This I did, but the lessons were usually a nightmare for me because Julian could not keep still at all, while everybody else's children seemed able to. He had an irritating way of doing things wrong on purpose and watching intently to see if he was creating the desired effect. When he found that he was he would roar with laughter and jump on and off his small stool while mother nearly died of embarrassment.

'Once Alison suggested that it might be "fun" to combine a lesson with another small pupil. My heart *sank*. There was nothing I could do about it. But Julian thought it was hilarious, especially when they played together and were told to count when they had bars of rests. He found that by counting at a slightly different time he could upset the proceedings in a profoundly satisfactory manner. The final straw came when his excitement reached fever pitch and, leaping on to the stool, he started attacking the other child with his bow in an elaborate fencing motion at which point Alison screamed in horror "Julian, dear, it's your precious bow, not a sword!"

'Nevertheless, he redeemed his reputation at one of the periodical concerts held in a hall in Duke Street, when he played a short piece from his very first solo book, dressed in a pale blue silk shirt and navy velvet shorts. This completely captivated the audience, and one man was heard to remark "Oh isn't he *divine*".

'Actually he played quite well too and, for once, seemed to be concentrating!

'Another agonising occasion was his Grade 1 exam. He was five at the time and so small we had to take his stool with him as the chairs were too high. We made our way to the Royal Academy and I accompanied him for his pieces. The examiner was very serious and not in the least amused by this small apparition. He played from memory so there was no question of his having to use the large wooden stands which would not go lower than a certain height. When the exam finished Julian appeared and seemed highly satisfied with his performance. I asked him about the sight-reading, imagining that the examiner would have held it for him or put it on a chair at a suitable height.

' "Oh! I couldn't see *that*," said Julian casually, "it was on the stand and it was much too high."

' "What did you do, then?" I asked nervously.

' "Oh, I just made it up," said Julian — "it was quite all right."

'The marks for that section did not bear out this extreme self-confidence, but for once it was not his fault.'

I must have done a certain amount of work for when I was nine I joined my brother at the Saturday morning Royal College of Music Junior Department. This was a great excitement for me as not only would I be learning the cello with a very good teacher called Rhuna Martin (wife of the flute-player William Bennett) but I would also be expected to start on a second instrument. As a performance of Haydn's Military Symphony was being mounted by the College orchestra at the time, both Andrew and I chose to do percussion, as this would mean us being immediately drafted into it. Andrew played cymbals and I played the bass drum, or *Gran Cassa* as it seemed to be called on the orchestral parts. The whole episode can have done little for Carleton Hobbs's concentration on his Sherlock Holmes scripts as it necessitated an immense amount of home practice on these deafening instruments.

By an amazing chance, this encounter with the orchestral percussion led to my introducing to the family someone who was to become one of our closest friends — the pianist John Lill. Then only seventeen but later winner of one of the world's most sought-after music prizes — the Tchaikovsky International Piano Competition — John was playing timps in the orchestra. Few people know of his prowess at the timps. He was quite the loudest drummer

4

I've ever heard (including Jon Hiseman and Ginger Baker) and later went on to play in the Royal College's Senior Department orchestra. I have it on good authority that after the immense drum roll in the first movement of Beethoven's *Choral Symphony* (which is usually played by a relay of timpanists but which John, of course, did on his own) the entire brass section, who unfortunately sit only a few inches in front, were deafened for a week!

Strangely the star student at Junior College took an interest in me and it wasn't long before I asked him to come home and meet my parents. We took to him at once and he would amuse us with his party trick which was to look at a piece of music, then go straight to the piano and play it from memory. My mother, in particular, took a lot of interest in John who seemed to become almost like another son to her.

Andrew, three years my elder, was thirteen at the time. Did the sudden arrival on the scene of a visibly brilliant seventeen-year-old classical musician act as a spur to him?

It was this association with the Lill family that led to my supporting Orient Football Club and, indirectly, winning a gold disc for my pains. John came from Leyton in London's East End, and every Saturday afternoon after College was finished, my mother would drop John home and call on his mother with me in tow. This got a bit boring for a ten-year-old so, while they were nattering away, I'd go and see the O's who, believe it or not, were in the *First Division* at the time (*and* we beat Liverpool!). Week after week we would lose, and it was this underlying sympathy for the underdog which began my support for the Orient.

At the same time I was really beginning to enjoy my cello playing. Rhuna Martin was the sort of teacher I responded to. She talked about *music*, not technique, and at the time that was what I wanted to hear. We got stuck into major cello music — Bruch's *Kol Nidrei* and the Brahms *E Minor Sonata* — doubtless far too soon, but I loved it. She also took me to hear the first good cellist I ever heard — Pierre Fournier.

I was transfixed. I didn't believe it was possible to play the cello that way.

'I'll never play like that,' I complained.

'You will,' she replied.

I never believed her, but it was nice to feel that the person who watched, listened and guided me each week felt such confidence in me — she was giving me the encouragement I needed.

My precociousness on the cello had obviously been noted by the powers-that-be at College as I was invited to perform a solo at one of their end-of-term concerts and these were normally reserved for players quite a lot older. This was a big chance for me, so I pulled off the enormous coup of persuading John Lill to accompany me on the piano, and as the great day drew near I reached a fever of nervous anticipation.

I don't think John has ever quite forgiven me for what happened.

It was decided I should play the *Tarantella* by Squire — a fast and frantic piece with a piano introduction before the cello comes in. The dignified Royal College of Music concert hall was packed with people who had come specially to see their star pianist accompany this dreadful little boy in short trousers, but unfortunately the whole thing proved too much for me — with catastrophic results. In the heat of the moment I was convinced John had started off much too fast and after a few bars I stopped, swung round to the piano and cried in a loud, squeaky voice:

'Start again, it's too fast!'

He had no alternative, and so, with a look on his face that would have frozen the Equator solid and to the vast amusement of the entire audience, the future Tchaikovsky competition winner was forced to begin all over again at an altogether statelier pace. The piece ended to tumultuous applause but John was never allowed to live the episode down. To this day, when he proudly boasts never to have stopped during one of his concerts, there's always someone who'll pipe up 'But don't you remember the Squire *Tarantella*?'

I'm afraid he does.

Much as I was really beginning to enjoy playing, I certainly didn't see why I should be expected to practise all the time, especially on holiday. One summer we were all set to go off to Norfolk for a few weeks. My parents were insisting that I should take the cello and I was insisting I shouldn't – on the entirely reasonable grounds that daily practice could in no way be considered a proper holiday. However, reason did not prevail, I ran out of arguments and the matter seemed to be closed – the cello was coming too.

I decided something would be done and retreated to plan my next move. Running away was definitely out – that would merely postpone our departure, and I had tormented visions of myself locked in a room with the cello while everybody else was having fun. I thought of breaking the cello strings, but since they were instantly replaceable that was not a good solution. The whole situation called for something drastic and I quickly hatched an evil scheme.

There would be a Terrible Accident.

I picked up my bow and looked at it. There was no doubt this course of action was a touch extreme but I could think of no other way which would be quite so certain or, I feared, so final. I sat down, still holding it, trying to will myself into snapping it and began to feel a delicious sense of naughtiness creeping over me, becoming more and more exciting, eating away at my non-existent resistance until I had almost forgotten the reason. I just had to do it. I cracked the bow across my knee. Disappointingly, the noise was not quite as loud as I'd expected – just enough to temper my glee with horror.

Not only had I committed the act, now I had to get away with it. Without giving myself time to allow the enormity of it all to sink in, I rushed to my mother — broken bow in hand.

'Look what's happened. I didn't realise it was there and I sat on it.'

There was an awful silence during which I realised I was just as shocked as she was, but I could tell from her face that she couldn't possibly imagine her little boy had done something quite so dreadful on purpose.

My extra enjoyment of the holiday was only slightly tinged with shame, and that soon disappeared when the bow returned from the repairers with hardly a sign of its ghastly mishap. I still have it. In fact I still use it from time to time, but I never take it on holiday.

When I was ten my father was appointed Director of the London College of Music after spending many years as a professor at the Royal College. I believe the London College was at a pretty low ebb at this time, especially financially, and my father seemed extremely worried about the whole thing. But it can't have been all bad — the flute teacher was Jimmy Galway!

I clearly remember that at ten or eleven nothing could have been further from my mind than taking music up as a profession. I loved playing the cello, but it was for fun and I never practised properly — although I somehow managed to scrape through all the various exams. Musically I felt close to my brother in some ways and he used to bring home all the latest hit records from Bill Haley and Elvis to my own favourite of the time, Bobby Vee.

Even so I did seem to have developed a highly unusual interest in music written for the cello. In those days the *Radio Times* used to print a section of music broadcasts from foreign radio stations, and I would comb this through avidly in the hope of catching an unknown cello concerto by composers like Pipkov or Dukelsky (yes, they do exist!). Many a pirated recording was taped this way — intermittent cracklings and splutterings permitting. I built up an enormous collection of cello tapes and would start trying to struggle through music by Prokofiev and Shostakovich that was technically way beyond what I had been taught at that time.

My uncle, who lived in Italy, rather prided himself on his knowledge of classical music, so around this time Andrew and I decided to play a little trick on him. Inspired by a particularly discordant piece for solo cello by George Crumb, which we'd heard on the radio, we decided to compile a tape of 'a new masterpiece' for cello and piano which we would say we'd taped off the radio. It was called *Spasms for cello and piano* by Lloyd-Crumb and consisted of random bangings and grindings that crescendoed to a huge climax which then exploded into a massive *Monastery-Garden*-type tune.

It was our one and only joint compositional attempt and was met by a brief letter saying uncle had not enjoyed the piece but thought my cello-playing had come on a lot.

Despite grabbing every opportunity I could to hear cellists play in London, I still had no intention of taking up the instrument myself.

At about thirteen all that changed.

Several things happened at once. Firstly, I heard the great Russian cellist Rostropovich for the first time when he came to London to give a series of nine concerts with the London Symphony Orchestra. This was announced as being 'the complete repertoire for cello and orchestra' although, even then I was annoyed at the concertos which were left out — no Delius, Walton or Khatchaturian. But it was a turning point. No other performer had made that kind of impact on me and I went to all nine concerts. In the programme Rostropovich wrote: 'The cello, without losing its power to express lyrical emotions and moods, has become in our times a tribune, an orator, a dramatic hero.' Rostropovich seemed to be acting as an ambassador for the cello and this struck an immediate chord within me.

I was also inspired by going to a new teacher — the late, great Douglas Cameron. He was responsible for teaching a whole generation of British cellists, including the present principal cellists of three of the four London orchestras, but perhaps his greatest achievement was in 1967 when the BBC held their only ever cello competition. Out of the four finalists no less than three, including the winner, were Cameron pupils. He also founded a Cello Club in London at which he managed to persuade many of the world's top cellists to come and play for no fee at all — quite an accomplishment! Among these were Rostropovich, Paul Tortelier, Zara Nelsova and Sir John Barbirolli.

So spurred on by the example of Rostropovich and the inspiration of Douglas Cameron, together with the fact that I was fast realising there was nothing else I'd ever really wanted to do, I decided I would be a solo cellist.

There was no question in my mind of becoming an orchestral player. I knew I could never take all those orders from all those conductors! As far as I was concerned I would be a solo cellist or no cellist at all. But I had a vast amount of catching up to do. Technically my playing must have lagged far behind that of other thirteen-year-old sons and daughters who had presumably been good little children and got on with their practice.

From the start I discovered it was considered — even by Douglas Cameron — an almost impossible task to become a solo cellist. I suppose he had watched too many of his pupils have a go at it over the years only to end up sadly disillusioned. My father also strongly advised me against entering the music profession, saying I should only do music on condition there was nothing else I thought I could manage to do. He told Andrew the same and I believe he was right — it's what I would tell someone of thirteen myself now.

My father's thinking was that music is such a tough and difficult profession to succeed in that only those who are prepared to fight against all the odds will manage it. The more I was told it was impossible to become a solo cellist the more I wanted to take up the challenge. They don't know what they're talking about, I would think to myself —

after all, look at Rostropovich. It was this determined, if naïve, attitude which was to help me through my next ten years and the rounds of London music agents who were all to say the same thing — there's no work for a solo cellist.

I think Douglas Cameron must have been surprised at my change in attitude during my first lessons with him. Although still at school, I would rush home and practise the cello with real enthusiasm for the first time. When he suggested that I learned the Shostakovich Sonata, I insisted on tackling the much harder Concerto instead. He said I wasn't ready for it. I told him to let me bring both pieces the next week and he could judge again for himself. Not surprisingly I made sure he let me get on with the Concerto, and at sixteen I won scholarships to both the Royal College and Royal Academy playing the Shostakovich and Boccherini Concertos on each occasion.

My schoolfriends must certainly have found me a bit odd round about this time because suddenly I was no longer going with them to films and parties but staying at home quite voluntarily to practise the cello. From thirteen to sixteen I was at University College School, Hampstead. It could hardly be described as a musical school (the music master at the time also doubled as the gym teacher), but I greatly enjoyed myself there all the same and my peculiar habit of locking myself into my bedroom and scratching away at my massive instrument for hours on end was, on the whole, tolerated with puzzled good humour.

Douglas Cameron was an unbelievable character. I think a lot of people who knew him, but didn't know his teaching, would have wondered how on earth he got such good results from his students, for he cut an extraordinary figure. He was a tiny, red-faced, rotund old Scotsman, and to say he liked a drink would be the musical understatement of the century. The trick was to make sure the lessons were first thing in the morning when last night's excesses had more or less worn off and the new day's had hardly begun.

13

His whole approach to teaching was based on the idea of trying to bring the best out of each individual rather than to impose any rigid style of playing. I remember there was one time when Paul Tortelier, who, of course, is famed for his own television master classes, went to judge a competition at the Royal Academy, where Cameron was professor. By chance it turned out that all the competitors that year were Cameron pupils. Tortelier was interested to know who their different teachers were as the standard had been so high. He could hardly believe it when he learned they were all with the same professor.

I think a general criticism of music teaching would be that most performers encourage their pupils to play in exactly the same way as they do, something which is neatly illustrated by a story from another famous cellist, Gregor Piatigorsky, who had this to report on his first encounter with the German professor Hugo Becker:

'Becker took his cello and said "We have to be frank, and I expect you to express your opinions freely. I will play the beginning of the Dvořák Concerto — only the beginning. After I have played, you will do the same. Then we will discuss the merit of each performance."

'He began. I saw a gust of resin fly, rise and fall in all directions. Ripping off the hair, his bow knocked on the sides of the cello. The stick hit the strings. After some noisy thumping on the fingerboard with his left hand, he stopped. I did not dare look at him. He asked something. His voice sounded happy. I looked at his face and saw that he *was* happy.

' "How did you like it?" asked Becker.

' "It was terrible," I said.

' "Heraus!" Becker screamed. "Out of here, you conceited, ignorant mujik!." '

Whatever they may say, the truth is that the majority of performers seem to like their pupils to copy them. If you play a concerto like they do it's musical and if you don't it's not musical. It was the very absence of such conceit that made Cameron an outstanding teacher.

Occasionally he could be too kind. I remember one day when I made the dreadful mistake of fixing a lesson for the afternoon. I arrived at his house with some trepidation at about 3.00 but there was no reply. Eventually, after repeated ringings, Douggie (as he was fondly known to everyone) lurched to the door and let me in. He was in a terrible state, for apparently his previous pupil had asked him straight out whether he thought he was good enough to make it as a soloist and Douggie, having had even more whisky than usual, had said that he didn't think so. I said I thought he had done the kindest thing, but Cameron obviously felt very bad about it and there was a terrible atmosphere of depression. Considerably more whisky flowed throughout my 'lesson' during which he fell asleep, woke up with a start, called me Gayle (the name of a delightful blonde girl he was teaching at the time) and dozed off to sleep again. Eventually I gave up, packed the cello and crept out of the house.

Douglas and his wife Lilly (also a cellist) had a terrific devotion to the cello. I, too, felt the same way about the instrument and when, at seventeen, the time came to leave him I felt very sad. I shall always regard him as my true teacher.

In April 1968 I was faced with an embarrassment of riches; the choice of scholarships to both of London's Royal music colleges. Should I choose the Royal Academy, where Douglas Cameron was the professor, or the Royal College where of course my father had been a professor for years? It was an agonising choice. In the end I decided a change might be a good thing for my playing. After three years with Douggie I felt I had understood and absorbed his approach to the cello and that a change of outlook could only be to the good, so I chose the College scholarship and the very different approach of Joan Dickson. Later on I regretted not having worked with Douggie full-time. All our lessons had been while I was still at school and there was so much music I would like to have covered with him. I made up for this later by regularly playing things over to him right up to his death in 1974.

Just before entering the RCM I gave what turned out to

be my last concert under his tuition. It was very much a family affair held at Central Hall, Westminster, where my father was the organist. Andrew had written a piece with his new lyricist Tim Rice based on the Bible story of Joseph and his coat of many colours. It had gone well at its first performance at Colet Court boys' school and they decided it should receive a more public airing. So a concert was arranged in aid of the new drug-addiction centre, which had just been set up at Central Hall. It featured John Lill, my father on the organ, and the public première of *Joseph and the Amazing Technicolor Dreamcoat*, as it was now called. I was to play the Saint-Saëns Concerto.

A lot of interest grew in the event and on the night the hall was packed with an audience of nearly three thousand. I had never played in front of anything like this number of people before and was scared limp by the whole proceedings. I thought I had played unbelievably badly, and my first concert review in a national newspaper resulted in my first disagreement with a critic. *The Times* described it as 'a superb account of the concerto'.

I was thoroughly depressed afterwards, but as I beat a hasty retreat via the Hall's back door I encountered what I suppose could be described as my first fan. Armed with her autograph book was an excited, waif-like little blonde girl of about fifteen or sixteen.

'You were brilliant,' she giggled as my shaky hand attempted a signature.

'Thank you,' I stuttered, feeling about a hundred times better already.

We set off on our different ways, but turning the corner I glanced quickly back at the fast-disappearing figure who six years later was to become my wife.

Not only the skirts were high when I began my student days at the Royal College. It was September '68 — the end of the 'Swinging Sixties' when London was *the* place to be, party-going the order of the day and — truth be told — not a lot of work got done. At college most of the time seemed to be spent in Room 99. This was the pub around the corner and acquired its affectionate nickname, 'The 99', as the College originally had 98 rooms. (When the new building appeared, its room numbers tactfully began at 100.)

At any given time there are approximately 800 students at the RCM, so if you add to these all the other students from all the other British music colleges, it is pretty obvious that each July an awful lot of young musicians are going to be looking for work in an already vastly overcrowded profession.

Surprisingly, I always had the impression that the students who worked at college were in a minority and on the whole viewed with deep suspicion by most of their contemporaries, many of whom seemed to find music a chore rather than a voyage of discovery. Perhaps I was lucky to have a conversation with one of my former teachers, Rhuna Martin, just before arriving there. She had been a student at the College and told me that the three, or, at the most, four years I had there would be the only time when I could just practise and work at the cello without having to worry about giving concerts, earning a living, and all the other paraphernalia which surrounds a soloist; that it was not possible to go out into the profession only to decide after a couple of years you were not good enough and needed another three or four years' study. It was my only chance so I must not waste it.

Looking back I think I followed her advice with surprisingly few lapses and even these probably helped my cello playing. After all, how can you interpret music if you don't have an understanding of life? As Peter Skellern's professor said to him after Peter had played some Debussy rather innocently at his weekly piano lesson:

'Come back next week and play it again when you're no longer a virgin.' I'm told Peter obliged on both counts!

At the end of your time at college you take an associate diploma either in performing or teaching. You can enter for this qualification whether you're at the College or not, and I had taken and passed my performer's diploma the autumn *before* going there. This meant that I never had a diploma to work towards while studying. So I was always looking beyond the RCM's stately corridors towards the musical world outside.

Apart from the fact that they both played cello, about the only thing my new professor Joan Dickson had in common with Douglas Cameron was his race. She certainly didn't share her fellow Scotsman's enthusiasm for whisky and her strict, intense method of teaching could not have been more contrasted with Cameron's relaxed (one could almost say 'laid back') style. Although I didn't always appreciate it at the time, her disciplined approach did me a lot of good and we covered a great deal of music in our two years together. Many of her lessons were given as 'master-classes' — in other words, in front of an audience. In the wrong hands I've always thought the 'master-class' can turn out to be another excuse for the so-called 'master' to have a big ego-trip — usually at the expense of some poor, unfortunate student who is often too nervous to answer back. I remember a master-class when a certain French maestro was coaching a particularly delectable blonde student on

18

the Dvořák concerto. As soon as she'd arrived at a suitably passionate passage he interrupted.

'You play like a virgin!' There was a little pause before he continued: 'You are a virgin, yes?.'

While most of the male audience gripped the edge of their seats awaiting the reply, she merely blushed in embarrassed silence. What they, and presumably the maestro, didn't know was that the girl's husband was sitting in the front row.

Rostropovich is another who certainly doesn't mince words:

'Your vibrato is like a goat,' he told one miserable-looking boy. 'Open window on your playing and let fresh air in.'

The boy began once again only to be halted abruptly:

'Ah, I see you've opened window, but air coming in is polluted!.'

The prize for the most devastating remark, however, must go to the violinist Sidney Griller — a brilliant player who gave his name to the legendary Griller String Quartet. As a teacher he has a reputation that lives up to his name. A complete opposite to the kindly, easy-going Douglas Cameron, he is quite capable of tearing a player apart as he did one quartet lesson. Stopping us mid-phrase he enquired of the first violinist:

'How old are you?'

'Twenty-three,' came the puzzled reply.

An awful silence descended while Griller paced the room.

'Oh,' he intoned sadly, 'I thought you were about sixteen. With a lot of work you might have had a bright future.'

You could say he was being cruel to be kind.

Having given these classes myself now, I can see only too easily the temptation to put on a show for the audience, who will often expect it. Certainly Joan Dickson, a most unassuming and modest person, could never have been accused of doing that. She preferred to call her classes 'workshops' and only other cellists were encouraged to attend. Even so I found the class system difficult and it was only afterwards that I realised just how good a preparation

19

it had been for the profession. I used to be petrified during my classes (after all, other cellists don't necessarily make the sweetest audience) and they were the first regular experience I had of playing in front of other people. Each class I would develop all those symptoms that give a soloist recurring nightmares. My left hand fingers would start sweating profusely and I'd slide to all the wrong notes. My concentration would suddenly disappear and I'd forget all my hard-learned fingerings. I'd suddenly get cramp in my legs and have to twist around the chair like a demented snake and my right hand would start to shake, sending the bow shuddering and trembling along the strings. The last of these symptoms ('the pearlies' it's called in the profession) is definitely the worst — a special nightmare all the string-players' own. For the more you try to stop the bow shaking, the more it shakes and in the end you find you've dropped the wretched thing altogether.

Although it certainly did not feel like it then, this was the best possible preparation for concert-giving as I was forced to discover methods of controlling my nervousness. The best way of doing this is the most obvious — you should lose yourself totally in the music so that the body becomes merely a channel for it to flow through. If the mind is given completely to something outside the physical body, nerves disappear. Although part of the mind has to be aware of its physical surroundings, the technical sides of a performance should have been prepared before, leaving the music to take control.

Unless you are incredibly lucky this condition can only be achieved by practice of performance and the increasing confidence that experience should bring. There will naturally be days when nervousness seems to be getting the upper hand, but during my college classes I learned one or two specific ways of dealing with it. For example, when my right hand began shaking and the bow bounced all over the strings I would immediately focus attention on my left-hand fingerings — I'd forget about the bow and it would start to behave properly again.

There are many such tricks for dealing with nerves and doubtless every performer has his own. It would be a curious artist who never suffered from this complaint as this surely implies a lack of feeling for the sense of occasion, which there must always be. I remember being very surprised when Sir Adrian Boult told me, towards the end of his active conducting days, that he could honestly say he was no longer nervous before concerts. I believe nerves can be made to work *for*, rather than against you — that extra flow of adrenalin sharpening the reflexes and giving each performance a special edge. Looking back, I'm grateful that I had this experience at college, which helped me to cope at the start of my career, but at the time I thought it was an insurmountable problem.

If classes were nerve-racking, orchestra was worse. A day or two after arriving at College I discovered I'd been made leader of the orchestra's cello section, which meant that every so often, in the middle of a symphony, a solo would come along. Surrounded by the vast sounds of an orchestra I'd turn over the page and see the dreaded word SOLO at the bottom, realising it would be only too soon that the rest of the cello section deserted me and I'd be left to suffer all on my own. The audience aren't expecting you to play by yourself and when it happens you can feel their eyes swivel in your direction with surprise and anticipation. It is a truly terrible moment which brings to mind a story of the violinist Kreisler, strolling along Lexington Avenue on the afternoon of a concert at Carnegie Hall. Suddenly he caught sight of a row of cod in a fishmonger's and, transfixed by their beady, staring eyes, cried out:
'My God, I'm supposed to be giving a concert this evening!'
I certainly wouldn't swap places with an orchestra's principal cellist for a second — I think I'd find his work far more frightening than mine.
Playing in the College orchestra did have its lighter moments. On one occasion a 'distinguished' professor of composition from a German university was foisted on us, as it had evidently been decided that we would learn a great deal from playing his latest piece. Unfortunately, the

21

mass of squiggles, arrows and circles on the page seemed to defy any kind of rational explanation and the professor's vain attempts to enlighten us, in faltering English, only made things worse. One sign apparently meant we were to bash the side of the instrument with our left hand while bowing on the wrong side of the bridge with the other. This, I should imagine, sounded a bit like a pack of wolves on heat (with drum accompaniment) and caused much merriment among the rest of the orchestra, which was unfortunately not shared by the professor, who by this time was distinguished only by his temper.

Certainly the piece was not of the greatest aural beauty and in the middle of one particularly dirge-like passage on the depths of the C string a voice from the back was distinctly heard to grumble:

'It sounds a bit like an incontinent fly.'

The disappearance of the entire cello section — by this time doubled up over their instruments — from the orchestral texture of his masterpiece caused the apoplectic German to fling his baton to the ground in an explosion of disgust. As leader of the section I bore the brunt of his wrath:

'Das iss ze musik off ze future!' he boomed. 'You vil not blame me ven you huff to play zis and do not know how should go!'

Roused by the indignities I'd been forced to inflict on my long-suffering cello all afternoon, I found myself shouting that I would rather starve than play his 'music' – well maybe I didn't say 'music', but in any case there didn't seem to be much point in hanging around, so I ceremoniously stormed off the platform followed by a convoy of fellow cellists — a magnificent victory for the Cellists' Liberation Front.

One undoubted compensation of orchestral playing is the companionship found among the players; a companionship you can never have as a soloist, when two ships quite often pass in the night but rarely dock in the same port.

The camaraderie of orchestral life was clearly brought home to me at the end of my first year at College. I was part of a group of students from the RCM who were hand-picked by a certain conductor to tour Austria as a 'baroque ensemble' during the summer holidays. Although we weren't actually going to make money, it seemed a marvellous chance to tour Austria on an all-expenses-paid trip, while, for his part, he obviously thought it would be a great way to make his name and that he'd be returning to London with a sheaf of glowing reviews under his arm.

But he wasn't up to it. We had endless rehearsals — mostly for his benefit — before leaving, but every time we stepped on to the platform there was a feeling that anything could happen.

Somehow we staggered through the first couple of concerts without any major catastrophies, but at the third disaster struck. The conductor seemed more than usually hesitant right from the start and each beat was a miracle of indecision. A calamity was unstoppable and sure enough when we got to the end of a section which was supposed to be repeated, he changed time and went straight on.

Panic ensued.

Some of us ploughed on while others went back, instantly transforming Vivaldi to cacophany. There might have been a chance to retrieve the situation, but, instead of simply saying 'Go on' or 'Go back', the floundering figure on the rostrum cried out 'No!'.

The silence was shattering.

A trumpeter came in *fortissimo* by himself.

'No!' he blustered hysterically.

Everything stopped. Someone went on, others went back again, and I'll never know how we got to the end. Many of the orchestra were in tears afterwards — and there were still four concerts left to endure. But a spirit of adversity had already developed among the players which somehow saw us through. We decided the only way of getting to the end of each concert was to play the pieces ourselves and totally ignore any further directions from the crazed conductor — who by this time had resolved to give up music altogether the second he got home. It was a clear case of forced retirement.

Another first-year out-of-college date also ended in fiasco. The College was asked by the nearby Royal Court Theatre in Sloane Square to provide a couple of students to play in two performances of their new Congreve production. The parts were small — just two short pieces for oboe, cello and harpsichord — but we would be on stage and required to wear period costume (wigs and all). The Royal Court had already found a harpsichordist so the College despatched Roy Carter (a fine oboist) and me, obviously thinking it would be very good experience for the pair of us.

On the afternoon of the first performance we apprehensively went along to our one and only rehearsal, but everything seemed pretty straightforward. We had one piece to play in the first half, another in the second, returning at the end to take our bows with the rest of the cast. In fact, we rehearsed the bowing a lot more than the playing — the harpsichordist was supposed to kneel in front of us while Roy and myself stood ceremoniously behind. The hardest part of the evening for me was trying to manoeuvre my cello down the dark, narrow staircase which led from dressing-room to stage.

The first show went fine and I think we both felt rather pleased with our theatrical débuts, even if the wigs and flowing robes were stifling to play in. By the second night we'd become a bit blasé about the whole thing and decided to have a little game of cards to kill time between the two pieces — keeping one ear on the dressing-room speaker which the management had thoughtfully provided to give us our cue. Needless to say we missed it.

We both heard the fateful words which were supposed to herald our grand entrance at the same moment. Roy jumped up, grabbing his oboe, and plunged two at a time down the lethal staircase. Unfortunately, I could not be quite so mobile.

By the time I'd manoeuvred my unwieldy instrument in the vague direction of the stage it was too late to go on. Roy, however, was there — oboe at the ready — when he heard me clattering and panting desperately behind. As he caught sight of my distraught bewigged face in the wings the whole episode finally got the better of him and he choked convulsively over his oboe. Apparently my dash to the stage was heard by the entire audience and I slunk on to take my final curtain-call with a feeling of embarrassment which became more acute the more the audience cheered and whistled my arrival.

Ill-luck struck again.

As we were taking our bows I'd failed to notice, until too late, that my cello spike had become inextricably entwined among the kneeling harpsichordist's flowing robes, effectively pinning him to the stage. Before I could do anything about it he rose with a flourish, rending his costly cloak in two and sending me diving after the ricocheting cello. Everyone fell about laughing.

The Royal Court management was not so amused. Apart from ruining their production, we'd obviously stolen the show, and I crept into College next day expecting to be immediately summoned before the Director. But, incredibly, nothing more was ever heard from the theatre — maybe they'd had a sudden surge of bookings?

The RCM was a curious place to study — I remember all the instrumentalists had their own tables in the canteen — a rowdy one for the brass, a studious one for the organists and, obviously, a cultured one for the strings. But despite an atmosphere which alternated between extremes of lethargy and competitiveness, I am very grateful for my time there.

There is a school of thought, nowadays, that seems to think it's much better for aspiring soloists either to study abroad or not go to college at all. Britain is a bit inclined to dismiss its music colleges with the sort of remark made by Sir Thomas Beecham, who declared that Benjamin Britten was 'the only worthwhile English composer to have emanated from one of our colleges of music'. (What about Holst and Vaughan Williams?) But the British school of cello playing has always been one of the best and I don't think I could have had a better teacher than Douglas Cameron. From Beatrice Harrison onwards, Britain has produced her fair share of fine cellists, and it certainly doesn't follow that lots of trips to famous teachers abroad will produce a master. For me the 'year's study abroad', which many aspiring soloists seem to find obligatory, can be another excuse for putting off the eventual moment of truth on the concert platform. If there is an outstandingly talented student at music college, a sort of buzz begins to

26

grow inside the profession and music agents wait in the wings to be first in for his signature. Often, during that 'year's study abroad', the buzz disappears. By the time he returns home, thinking everyone's waiting patiently for him, he's been forgotten and the attention has wandered on to some other potential star.

No amount of lessons can be a substitute for the real experience of giving concerts, and it is only too easy to keep thinking you are not quite ready to make the début. The truth is, there is *always* more work that can be done, *always* something more to be learned, but eventually you have to set yourself a date and go through with it.

I tried as hard as possible to make sure there would already be some concerts in my diary when I left college so I gave my London début recital at the Wigmore Hall while still a student — hoping this would mean I had some good reviews with which to tackle the profession. I also did auditions for two further London concerts and one for a young artists series on Dutch television, as well as entering a competition administered by the Philharmonia Orchestra to take lessons from the great French cellist Pierre Fournier. If successful, this would mean I could combine concerts with further study.

Luckily, all these things came off, but in a sense I'd already had my big break via the College itself. I auditioned for their 'Concerto Trials' to perform the long and immensely difficult *Symphony-Concerto* by Prokofiev, and they decided that I should play the work in a special eightieth birthday celebration concert for the Master of the Queen's Musick, Sir Arthur Bliss. After the concert was over, Sir Arthur left a parcel for me with Sir Keith Falkner, the Director — it was an inscribed score of his own Cello Concerto.

I knew the Concerto had just been performed by my hero, Rostropovich, at the Aldeburgh Festival, and was delighted at the prospect of settling down to learn it myself over the summer holidays. Happy with my progress, I wrote to Sir Arthur asking if I could come and play it through to him — thinking he'd probably forgotten all about me.

Next morning the telephone rang and I heard an incredibly sprightly voice asking me if I could come and play his Concerto to him later that week!

With fear and trepidation I went along to his house in St John's Wood having hurriedly fixed someone to play the orchestral part on the piano. It was the first time I'd ever played a work through to its creator and I was convinced that the man who actually composed a piece was bound to be the most severe critic. I was wrong.

Sir Arthur seemed especially pleased I'd learned the Concerto from memory but, apart from that, hardly said a word. I honestly thought he might have disliked my performance so much that he didn't see the point of making further comment, and I left St John's Wood thoroughly depressed. I had enjoyed working on the Concerto but all that hard work now seemed a waste of time.

Within a few days the College term started and as I sat through Sir Keith Falkner's annual speech to the students I seriously contemplated giving the whole thing up. I had spent my whole summer holidays working on a Concerto I would never play. Maybe I just wasn't good enough.

My musings were interrupted by a sentence from the Director that made me wonder if I was still dreaming:

'. . . and Julian played it "like the British Rostropovich".'

As the full story of Sir Keith's meeting the day before with Sir Arthur Bliss emerged, I felt stunned and embarrassed. Apparently Sir Arthur had done nothing but enthuse over my playing. Not only that, he had suggested me for the work's first London performance a year later at the Queen Elizabeth Hall!

More than anything else, this premiere launched my career, and it would not have happened but for that initial performance at College.

Unknown to me, another legendary musical figure was in the audience that night — Mrs Emmie Tillett from Ibbs & Tillett concert agency. Over the years she had managed all the great names in music, from Casals and Rachmaninov onwards. A remarkable septuagenarian, she was outwardly one of the sweetest old ladies you could meet, but scratch the surface and you found solid steel. One did not argue with Emmie Tillett. I certainly didn't when I was commanded for an interview following the concert.

It felt strange sitting in her office surrounded by all those signed photos of legendary artists, but the meeting was a great success. She had been impressed by my playing and offered me management starting from the time I left College in summer 1972 — a year from then.

Another exciting College occasion was when the Director chose me to play Fauré's *Elegy* at 'The President's Concert' — the President being Her Majesty, Queen Elizabeth The Queen Mother. She was delightful to meet and, once again, I encountered Sir Arthur Bliss who astonished me by declaring he had never before heard the *Elegy* (one of the best-known of all cello solos).

Although this was an important concert for me, it was completely overshadowed by my impending début at the Wigmore Hall less than three weeks later. Nothing can ever quite equal the crescendo of excitement before your first 'official' public concert. This is the moment you have to prove you can do it, the moment when all the talk, the scholarships and the student success count for nothing. In London you play to one of the world's most sophisticated audiences, so used to their glittering array of passing musical stars that they almost take them for granted.

I chose my programme with immense care but with an audacity that frightens me now and, come to think of it, frightened me then. I wanted to show I could interpret the classics, i.e. Beethoven and Brahms, but I also wanted to include some British music. So between the final Beethoven Sonata and the great Brahms in F major, I played the Delius Sonata. Perhaps I had in mind Douglas Cameron's classic remark: 'Nothing's as good as the Ireland except, of course, the Delius.' Perhaps not. But I do know I was especially inspired during the Delius.

That night I couldn't sleep at all — I found myself going over the whole concert again and again. Could I have done such and such a thing better? Why did I make a certain mistake? Yes, that bit had gone well . . . . And then there was the terrifying prospect of the next day's newspapers.

Was I going to be torn apart, never to play in public again? Or was I going to get rave reviews and be an overnight success? Maybe they would be something in between. Perhaps one would be good, the other bad. Eventually I fell sound asleep at about 6 o'clock only to be woken by my mother clutching a *Daily Telegraph*.

The Times hadn't printed its review yet, but the *Telegraph* was good. I couldn't bear to look and got my mother to read it out.

'An exceptional talent, the 20-year-old cellist Julian Lloyd Webber made his first Wigmore Hall sonata recital last night a very distinguished affair.

'The rich adagio and the athletic fugue of Beethoven's Sonata in D major were marvellously integrated and balanced.

'An expansive account of the Delius Sonata brought out the opulence of the instrument . . . .

As she finished reading the review, I sat glowing on the bed — the world was truly a wonderful place. What I hadn't bargained for was the *Telegraph*'s policy, in those days, of letting their overnight subs make up the heading for each concert.

As my mother handed me the paper and I spotted the error, my heart sank. '*An exceptional talent*' proclaimed the headline — '*at the piano.*'

What no student can ever know is just what it is like touring the world with a cello. Had *I* known, I am sure the piccolo would have seemed infinitely more appealing on that fateful afternoon at the Festival Hall.

For as long as I can remember I have been surrounded by remarks like: 'Look out, he's got a machine gun', the slightly rarer, 'Bet you can't get *that* under your chin', and — most hackneyed of all: 'Give us a tune, mate.' But my first real taste of the travel problem came following a concert in Cambridgeshire in 1970.

It was a 'musical evening' with the television celebrity Richard Baker acting as master of ceremonies. When we'd finished I was presented — for reasons best known to the organisers — with two large but decidedly dead pheasants. These I placed on the back seat of my Mini alongside the cello. On the journey home I was stopped by the police.

'Are you aware, sir, that your left-side rear light is failing to function, which is an offence under regulation. . .?'

'No, it must have just gone — it was definitely working when I set out.'

'And what, sir, are you carrying in the back?' he continued ominously, peering through the window at the shadowy forms behind me.

'Two pheasants and a cello,' I replied confidently.

'May I remind you,' intoned the policeman in considerably sterner tones, 'that it is also an offence to obstruct a police officer in the course of his duty. I will ask you once again,' he crescendoed, 'what are you carrying in the back?'

At which point I got out and let the crestfallen officer discover the ugly truth for himself.

That little incident is one of only a few actual brushes with the police in defence of my cello, even though I was later to have a gun drawn on me by a security man at Kennedy Airport. But there's no doubt, however, that I would have spent at least a couple of nights in the company of the German *polizei* had they witnessed the disgraceful fracas that occurred during one rush-hour outside Frankfurt railway station.

Strangely — but by no means out of keeping with British musical life — I gave the first broadcast performance of Britten's *Third Cello Suite* for Frankfurt Radio, arranging to record it in the afternoon so that I could travel down to Munich the same evening. We were scheduled to have finished by 5.00 and I planned to catch the 6.00 train to Munich. It was a hot sweltering day and when the broadcast was over I felt tired and exhausted. By the time I left the studio, at about 5.15, rush-hour traffic was at a standstill and it seemed that the only way to make the station in time was to lug my suitcase and cello on to a tram. The first one that came was packed like the proverbial sardine can but somehow I squeezed on, trying desperately to protect my precious possession from the flailing arms and feet that seemed hell-bent on destroying it altogether.

The heat was unbearable, it was impossible to breathe and — even with my lack of German — I caught sound of some very rude words indeed. With every fresh lurch of the tram people toppled over the cello, and one man in particular seemed to think I should never have brought it on in the first place. Muttering oaths in respective languages we glared at each other furiously until the tram finally juddered to a standstill — hurling him towards me.

Now, any threat to the well-being of my instrument

32

requires speedy action, so I thrust my fist in the direction of his descending torso — solely to prevent a nasty accident. Obviously this was misconstrued, for instead of gratefully acknowledging my helping hand, he grabbed a nearby briefcase and flung it hard at the cello.

This was a mistake.

What little British reserve I still possessed went straight out of the tram window as the cowardly aggressor fled down the steps to what he thought was the safety of the passing throng. Snatching up my cello and case, I raced in pursuit. But chasing Germans who've attacked your cello, while carrying it and a heavy suitcase, had not been part of the College curriculum and he was streaking ahead. For all I knew the instrument was badly damaged and he wasn't getting away with it. With a last, magnificent burst of speed and propelled by the full weight of cello, suitcase and temper my right foot hit the escaping backside hard and true — sending him sprawling headlong to the pavement where he belonged.

After satisfying myself that the cello was still in one piece I ignored his whines about the police and proceeded — with the aid of a couple more beers than usual — happily on the journey to Munich, pleased with the day's varied exertions.

The train, in theory, is a cellist's least worrying form of transport although, even here, things are not what they used to be. Nostalgia freaks will instantly recall those single first-class compartments with the regal upholstery you could have all to yourself. Now virtually extinct, thanks to rapists, vandals, muggers and cost-cutting, they have been replaced by impersonal through-corridor coaches, virtually identical to the ones in second class. Worst of all, tables have been inserted between the seats, making it quite impossible to remove one's instrument for a quick fiddle, however deserted the rest of the carriage may be.

One day I had made myself lunch and was quietly ruminating over a copy of Arthur Machen's *Hill of Dreams* when the phone went. It was Andrew Green, my manager at Ibbs & Tillett.

33

'Tortelier's ill,' he said, 'and he's scheduled to play the Haydn D major in Nottingham. Will you do it?'

'When?' I asked, remembering it was a good year since I'd played it.

'Tonight. There's a train leaving at 1.50 — you should just make it. Oh, by the way, there's a rehearsal at 4.30.'

After rifling through the music cabinet for the Haydn I quickly stuffed my evening clothes in a case and set off for St Pancras in a state of mild delirium. By the time the taxi reached the station I'd decided to cancel the whole thing; totally unprepared there would be no time to practise one of the hardest concertos in the whole repertoire. I rang Ibbs from the station. They were engaged.

Re-dialling the number, I became increasingly distracted by the sight of the extraordinary old bone-shaker arriving on the Nottingham platform — complete with first-class compartments. Suddenly the problem had vanished. With any luck I'd be able to get in a good couple of hours' practice on the journey.

'Ibbs and Tillett,' interrupted the voice at the other end.

'. . . Er . . it's Julian here — just tell Andy I'm on my way.'

Only then did I realise I had dashed out with hardly any money and could only just rustle up a second-class fare. Still, the risk had to be taken and I plonked myself down in first class, unpacked the cello and set about practising the Haydn with a vengeance. Half way towards Luton and the end of the first movement, I heard the ticket inspector in the compartment behind.

Now what should I do — hide in the loo, leaving the cello behind on the seat? Yet again I wished I had chosen the piccolo and could have stuffed the wretched thing out of sight altogether. Somehow I was going to have to try and explain.

As the guard advanced I attacked the Haydn with renewed vigour, trying to look for all the world as if it was a perfectly natural thing to be doing on the train to Nottingham. For a moment he hesitated by the door. Glancing up I saw him gazing incredulously at the contents of his compartment and prepared for the worst. But instead

34

of coming in he shot off down the corridor, obviously convinced an escaped lunatic was aboard his train.

Meanwhile, I had discovered interesting new methods both of fare-dodging and of making sure you kept a compartment to yourself and returned happily to my Haydn.

A few years later these old trains came to my rescue again. Right in the middle of a hectic run of concerts I had one at the Festival Hall with Stephane Grappelli. We had worked together once before for television, but this time Stephane was suggesting pieces which were just names to me. Our concert was on a Thursday and the previous Sunday I had a Queen Elizabeth Hall recital followed by concerts in Dundee on the Monday and Glasgow on the Tuesday. We decided I should catch the first plane from Glasgow on Wednesday in order to spend the rest of the day rehearsing.

On Tuesday, before leaving Dundee, I phoned home only to be told that the BBC's *Nationwide* programme had asked us to pre-record a number next morning and that, naturally, they wanted something we hadn't done on TV before. Apparently they had decided on the old Django Reinhardt hit *Nuages*. For a seasoned jazzer like Stephane, who can improvise anything, any time, this kind of thing holds no terrors, but *I* didn't even know the tune!

In the forlorn hope they might have a copy of *Nuages* I quickly rang the only music shop I could trace.

'New Age, sir? Oh no, we don't stock punk, sir, there's not much call for it here in Dundee.'

'It's not punk,' I protested, 'it's an old tune for guitar by Django Reinhardt.'

'I can't say that I've ever heard of it myself, sir, but I'll go and have a look for you. What would it be under?'

'Guitar,' I replied desperately, shoving another 10p in the slot. Ominous creakings could be heard in the distance; I hoped they were the sounds of rarely-disturbed music cabinets being opened and shut. With horror I realised it was just the shopkeeper walking off.

Two 10p's later she returned.

'No, sir, it's as I thought, sir. We haven't got it,' she

35

crowed triumphantly. 'We've got one called *Nuages* though, but. . .'

'I'll be right over,' I interrupted.

Astounded by the find, I dashed to the shop and immediately realised why they had the music — their last delivery had obviously been around 1933 when *Nuages* was a hit.

I had struck it very lucky and did again at the station. There, complete with separate compartments, was an unbelievably rare species of train — a dinosaur of the railways built long before Django Reinhardt, let alone *Nuages*, had ever been thought of. It was obviously destined for extinction alongside the Scottish wildcat. But for me it more than served its purpose and by the time we reached Glasgow *Nuages* was well and truly in my blood.

In many ways I prefer to drive to concerts. It does away with all the bother of getting to and from the station and lugging a heavy instrument and suitcase about. By car I can go straight from front door to artists' entrance with the cello either sitting safely beside me (I must check the law on safety belts and cellos) or lying flat across the back seat if there is a human passenger as well. Going by car also enables me to get home after concerts, which is virtually impossible by train nowadays. Even from a comparatively close city like Birmingham the last train to London leaves before 9.30, and whenever possible I like to be back ready to practise next morning.

Unfortunately driving at night has its dangers, and I have lost count of the number of times concert organisers have reminded me of Dennis Brain's tragic death on the road. Falling asleep at the wheel is the main hazard, and for some time I solved this problem by running a Mini: however tired you may be, it is practically impossible to doze off in something so noisy and bumpy. The Mini was also great for parking at Orient among the football crowds. Now there are no crowds and, some would say, not much football either, I've finally switched to a bigger car both for a smoother ride and greater protection.

I was nearly killed in the Mini on two occasions. The first was after a Harrogate Festival recital. On a dark but, mercifully, dry night I set off down the fairly narrow country road that winds from Harrogate to Leeds and the M1. Coming to a straight section I was touching seventy when suddenly the headlights picked out an enormous wagon-load of hay completely blocking my carriageway. It had no rear lights. Wrenching the wheel to the right and praying there was nothing the other side, I knew if I hit the curb I was done for. I missed the lorry and the curb, but the car went out of control, swinging violently from side to side. Somehow I managed to steady it and breathlessly crawled on to Leeds wondering how the tyres hadn't burst. I should have gone back and taken the lorry's number — whoever left it there was a potential murderer.

My second escape was even more extraordinary, but this time my wife Celia was driving. Travelling to Oxford along the M40 we had just reached the point where the foul power station at Didcot — fully twenty miles away — scars the landscape. Just as we were overtaking a Datsun, it pulled out and hit the Mini — plunging us into a seventy-miles-an- hour spin in the middle of the motorway.

I have heard it said that when someone knows he is about to die, he sees his whole life flash before him in a few seconds. But I had, among many others, one overriding thought. With the last line of *Don't Look Now*, Daphne du Maurier captured my feelings exactly: 'What a bloody silly way to die.'

Apart from the effrontery of climbing through the shattered windows of an overturned, written-off Mini completely unhurt, the memory of what happened next is a continuing source of embarrassment. Instead of rushing to Celia — who also appeared to have emerged unscathed — I tore frantically at what was left of the door, dragged out my cello and gave it an immediate inspection on the central reservation. It was an appalling revelation of priorities I have yet to live down, and which surely qualifies for some novel form of divorce proceedings.

People are used to trains and planes being delayed, but if you are driving and things go wrong, somehow you feel

Relegated to the balcony at Harrington Court (aged 5)

A few of the Harrington Court brigade. L–R: John Lill, W.S. Lloyd Webber with Dmitri (Shostakovich) and Jean Lloyd Webber with Sergei (Prokofiev) (Photo: Methodist Recorder)

With Sir Arthur Bliss (Photo: David Ingham)

Surrounded by the children after my first performance at an Ernest Read concert
(Photo: Times Newspapers Ltd)

Giving a masterclass outside the Royal College of Music (Photo: Evening Standard)

Kissing the bride with best man Andrew (Photo: David Ingham)

'The proudest moment of my life' – *on the pitch at Brisbane Road*
(Photo: Tony Furby)

more to blame. I remember allowing plenty of time to drive to Birmingham for a lunch-hour recital, having already checked the motorway was clear. Just after passing a turn-off point (Milton Keynes?) I found all three lanes completely blocked by an accident and remained stationary for at least an hour and a half — unable to go backwards, forwards, off the road or to a phone. It is amazing how isolated you can feel on a busy motorway.

For a few months in the winter of 1978 it was virtually impossible to get to concerts in Britain at all, let alone on time. That horrendous period came about largely by courtesy of something quaintly called the 'Social Contract'. This was the 'special relationship' between the then Labour Government and the Trade Unions whereby the Unions ran the country and the Government gave them lots more money in return. But, like most marriages for money, things turned sour when the cash ran out and the resulting chaos was the worst that even Britain has seen in years. There was *no* heating, *no* oil, *no* petrol, *no* trains but plenty of pickets.

To make matters worse God had evidently come out in support of the Unions and it snowed mercilessly throughout the conflict. Sensible people stayed in bed trying to convince themselves the whole thing was a dreadful nightmare, but a few unfortunates still had to try getting from one place to another. I remember particularly one frantic crawl to Manchester Airport. Arriving late for my flight to London, I was told that the plane which was supposed to take us there hadn't even left London for Manchester, let alone started its return journey.

Now travelling by plane is when the real trouble starts! Basically the problem is this: if a cellist wants to take his instrument into the cabin he must pay an additional full passenger fare. It doesn't matter how empty a plane is, the cello must be put with all the other baggage, regardless of its value and the fact that it can be safely strapped on to a seat. Of course, once the instrument is in the hold the airlines accept no responsibility if it gets smashed to pieces — for the obvious reason that this is extremely likely.

The one noble exception to this heathen approach is British Midland Airways. Sadly, they tend to go from places like Coventry to Jersey (Wednesdays only) and are ruthlessly opposed by other airlines every time they apply to go somewhere more profitable.

Apparently in the good old days, twenty-five years or so ago, airlines were pleased to welcome a cellist on board their flights. Nowadays, in an age when air travel is commonplace, any passenger with a remotely out-of-the-ordinary request constitutes a severe disruption to the well-oiled 'take the money and run' machinery.

A few years back my cello was damaged on a flight to Dublin. Despite various prior phone calls and messages via the travel agents explaining that I would be travelling with a valuable instrument, I found, on arrival at the air terminal (and in my view terminal is the best word for anything to do with airports) that no-one connected with the flight knew anything about it. At the check-in desk I prepared for the all too familiar battle.

'Would it be all right if I keep my cello beside me — I know there are some empty seats?'

'Not without payment of a full fare,' came the inevitable po-faced response.

'But surely it could at least go half fare,' I pleaded. 'After all, it doesn't eat, drink *or* smoke and it's much quieter than other passengers — at least while it's in its case.'

It was no good. Even the request to see the cello loaded into the hold fell on deaf ears.

'We must have our rules,' droned the official. 'Once we let *you* bring your cello on, *every* passenger will want to.'

Musing quietly to myself on the likelihood of two hundred cello concertos being performed in Dublin on the same evening I decided I wasn't getting very far and stupidly gave in — a mistake never to be repeated.

Opening my case at the other end I found that the cello's heavy ebony fingerboard had completely broken off, and the instrument had only narrowly escaped being broken into pieces. The rest of the afternoon was spent rushing from one repairer to another (there *were* only two!) in order to try and get the instrument restored for the evening. But it was obviously impossible, and only the kindness of a member of the orchestra, who lent me her cello, avoided the concerto being cancelled.

Looking back, some of my many battles with airline officials seem almost farcical but at the time, invariably under the watchful gaze of all the other passengers, they can be acutely embarrassing. I'll never forget my arrival, late and breathless, for a flight back to London from Amsterdam's Schiphol Airport.

'You can't bring that thing on 'ere,' said the stewardess, pointing rudely at the cello. 'If we let you bring *that* on, the next passenger will want to bring a grand piano.'

'But,' I protested, 'a grand piano can't quite fit on a seat the same way.'

As everyone craned their necks to get a better view of the row, the stewardess delivered her crushing punch-line:

'Oh yes it can — there's a new kind you can get now that *folds up*.'

Then there was the Bulgarian metal detector incident. This time the customs official in Sofia insisted on running his device up and down the strings, whereupon they screeched with disapproval. It then took an immense amount of effort — including an impromptu performance of the Prelude from Bach's Suite No. 1 — to persuade him that my cello wasn't the container of a hidden arsenal. I have heard all sorts of arguments in favour of gut strings from players who prefer them to metal ones, but they have, as yet, failed to mention the man at Bulgarian customs.

By now you may well be asking if it would not be a lot easier to give way, admit defeat and buy a seat for the cello. But the astonishing truth is that even a fully paid-for seat will not guarantee the instrument a place in the cabin. A few years ago Rostropovich had booked two *first*-class seats — one for himself and one for his cello on a flight (once again) to Dublin. Cunningly, the airlines will not accept a booking stating simply Cello — it has to be Miss or Ms Cello. When Rostropovich's flight turned out to be full, Ms Cello had to make way for a passenger, thereby wrecking

41

his rehearsal plans and nearly causing the concert to be cancelled altogether.

Yet perhaps the most frustrating episode of all happened after I had forked out an extra $300 or so on a seat for the cello for a flight from New York to Heathrow. As my blood pressure soared dangerously, the stewardess eyed the cello and declared:

'Say — you didn't buy a seat for the banjo? We'd-a-let-ya bring it on for free.'

At Kennedy Airport the security staff are a law unto themselves. When I gave my New York début, at the acoustically superb Alice Tully Hall, I made special arrangements to give the now sadly defunct Laker Airways a free advertisement in the programme on condition that the cello was allowed on to the plane — not on a seat, but in the cupboard where the cabin staff put their coats. Despite a letter from the airline authorising me to take it on, I was stopped by a security man when my turn came to board the aircraft.

Quickly I produced the letter.

'Who's it from?' he snapped, shoving it aside.

'The airline.'

'That's got nothing to do with *me. I'm Security*, and you're not going past here with *that*.'

'But if you'll read the letter you can see everything's been arranged. . . .'

'Either check it in as baggage or stay behind. NEXT PASSENGER,' he bawled, and everyone started pushing past.

Incensed, I started down the ramp myself. Evidently unused to such blatant disregard of his inflated authority the official made a grab for the cello. I jerked free and rushed towards the plane.

'Freeze!' he yelled in true TV style.

Still walking, I glanced over my shoulder and was amazed to see him waving a gun at me. Rashly calculating that he wouldn't dare shoot, I continued my increasingly shaky descent towards the — for once — welcome sight of the

cabin crew. Explaining I was a bit worried about getting a
.38 calibre bullet in my back the captain reassured me:

'Oh, that's just Mike — you don't want to worry about
him, he often gets a bit touchy.'

Aside from the endless rows with airline officials, there is
also the awful possibility of losing your suitcase altogether,
along with all your dress clothes and music. Many is the
time when an artist's case has turned up in Tokyo instead
of Sydney, but — touch wood — it has never yet happened
to me. When it does I shall know what to do.

Barry Tuckwell, the horn player, arrived at Snape
Maltings minus everything he needed for our concert that
evening except his horn. The airline had succeeded in
mislaying his case *en route* from Amsterdam to Norwich
and were blaming the Dutch baggage handlers. By 1.00
they still said there was no chance of his case being found in
time. But, strangely, after someone at the Aldeburgh
Festival Office explained that an announcement mentioning
the airline would have to be made to the audience, the
suitcase miraculously materialised.

Despite all the hassles and worries of travelling with a cello, I consider myself immensely fortunate to have seen so much of the world so soon. One of the nicest things about being a visiting soloist is how anxious people are to make you feel at home and leave their countries with happy memories.

Occasionally this means things that should be mentioned are not. Apparently, I should never have walked the length of Sunset Boulevard at two o'clock in the morning after the première of *Variations* in Los Angeles. And how was I to know that Helsinki's shopping precincts are invaded by meths drinkers the second it gets dark?

On the other hand I have been warned off areas so emphatically that it has made me quite determined to visit them at the first opportunity. On the way to my hotel in São Paulo, the lady concert representative relayed in shocked tones what sin and degradation I was sure to find just a few blocks away if I took a certain direction.

'It's disgusting what goes on round there!' she grimaced knowingly, 'transvestites . . . drug addicts . . . homosexuals . . . teenage girls on the streets. . . .'

'Which way is it?' I said, desperately trying to keep the new note of interest out of my voice, 'so that I can be sure to avoid it.'

When you finally arrive in your hotel room there's a

fresh problem — where to put the cello. Many instruments have been stolen from hotel bedrooms and, of course, the managements will not accept any responsibility. Yet it is hardly possible to leave the cello in the hotel safe every time you want to go for a walk. My trick is to hide it behind the shower curtain where, hopefully, thieves are less likely to be on the lookout for valuables — but this, too, has its drawbacks. Many-a-time must impressionable room maids have thought there was about to be some terrible re-enactment of that scene from *Psycho* as they caught sight of the shadowy black form hiding in the shower. Then I worry there might be a ghastly mishap with the hotel's water system, resulting in one badly warped cello.

Certainly people who practise in hotel bedrooms are regarded with the deepest suspicion. Several room maids have disturbed me at work only to recoil in horror as if I'd been caught performing some unmentionable act.

One particularly funny episode involved the wondrous device sometimes used by string players called a 'Dampit'. This contraption is designed to fight the devastating effects of central heating on old instruments which, at its most aggressive, dries out the atmosphere to such an extent that the wood splits apart. Basically the 'Dampit' consists of a thin length of hollow rubber tubing with holes down the sides and an absorbent piece of sponge in the middle. This you soak to a certain point, depending on the humidity, then insert down the instrument's 'f' hole. Unfortunately, to an untrained eye, the Dampit's purpose is by no means immediately apparent, and its discovery among the bed-clothes in my Brussels hotel room one morning caused the maid such hysterics that she flung it wildly in the air and ran, screaming, from the room leaving me to wonder what unspeakable use her rampant imagination had invented for the innocent appliance.

Much of my time on foreign tours is spent alone, for basically that is the way I prefer it when I'm working, but there are happy exceptions when a firm friendship is made many miles from home.

During my New Zealand tour in April 1983 Julian Bream was not only touring at the same time with the same orchestra but also, like myself, playing a Rodrigo Concerto. To add to the confusion we stayed at the same hotels throughout, but several delightful hours (and bottles of New Zealand wine!) were spent in his company.

For sheer chaos it would be hard to beat my Bulgarian tour of 1976. Things began to go wrong the moment I encountered the customs man and his metal detector.

Having survived this hiccup, I was mystified that no fewer than five empty taxis sped off as soon as I tried to hire them. Assuming it must be something to do with my Western appearance, I rapidly set about the monumental task of trying to do something about it until my interpreter assured me that, being on a state salary, taxi drivers do not need the trade and cannot be bothered with bulky objects like a cello.

After a check-in procedure obviously designed to make you believe you were really staying at the Kremlin, I was finally allowed to the supposed safety of my hotel room.

Three things were immediately apparent: the room was bugged, the loo didn't work and — worst of all — there were no curtains.

The first problem was easily solved. Unpacking my transistor radio, I tuned carefully to Radio Moscow and shoved it up against the microphone.

The loo was an altogether tougher proposition which proved — unfortunately — untreatable, along with the sewage. Certainly I would not be insulting my cello by hiding it *there*.

However, the curtains, or rather lack of them were the worst problem. If there's one thing that I need to sleep it is curtains. With a busy main street outside, powerful yellow floodlights illuminating the hotel's façade (and what's more, apparently reaching a massive climax at my window), sleep was clearly going to prove impossible.

Repeated attempts to get some curtains installed failed miserably and, in a desperate bid to block out the light, I started pinning up my clothes. But the windows stretched from an unusually high ceiling right down to the floor and by the time I'd finished, my entire wardrobe was on display to the citizens of Sofia.

From outside the view was incredible. My tailcoat hung upside down like a demented vampire and various bits of underwear were employed blocking up odd little chinks of light. Trouble was inevitable, but I adamantly refused to take my trousers down until a suitable substitute had been provided. Surprisingly, the ruse worked, and in no time at all a porter arrived clutching a pair of curtains.

Musically the tour was more successful. With the excellent Bulgarian pianist, Gyorgy Popov, I played sonatas by Vivaldi, Britten and Brahms. The night before arriving in Sofia I had played the same Brahms for a live broadcast in Hamburg with a German pianist. To work on successive days at the same piece with a German and a Bulgarian — neither of whom spoke a word of English — brought home very strongly what a wonderfully international language music is. Of course Italian terms are used in rehearsal, but really the music does all the talking.

Even though the concerts themselves were highly successful, with fine pianos and a lovely new hall to play in at Plovdiv — Bulgaria's second largest city — everything was extremely disorganised and we were constantly being given wrong travel and rehearsal times. At our final concert in the resort town of Borgas, inefficiency reached a new peak.

We arrived, as usual, in plenty of time for our 7.30 start and went for a little stroll beside the Black Sea. Spotting a poster for the concert we wandered over to have a look. The interpreter let out a shriek as he caught sight of the advertised starting time of 3.00!

It was already ten past, but — apart from leaving the audience awaiting our entrance — there was nothing for it but to dash to the hall and we took the stage drenched with sweat before we had even started!

A fraught two hours later I was confronted with the extraordinary problem of how to spend a lot of money very quickly which, at 5.45 in Borgas, is harder than you'd think. I was not allowed to take my fees out of Bulgaria so I had the alternative of either banking the money, in case I wanted to go back for a holiday, or spending it there and then. I had already seen quite enough to choose the latter, but my flight from Sofia left at 8.00 next morning and the promoters had cunningly waited until the final bars were over before I got paid.

My interpreter came up with the solution. Guiding me to an old part of the town we stumbled on an oasis of little shops and bazaars, one of which had a suspiciously large selection of Japanese watches. After buying several of the most expensive we decided on a celebration drink. Minutes later I was wishing we hadn't. Exploring down by the docks, he chose a dingy old bar full of sailors, specially, so he said, because of the beer. Accustomed to such superb brews as Fuller's London Pride and Ringwood's Old Thumper it was not long before I felt obliged to voice my opinion of the obnoxious fluid. This sent him into such fits of uncontrollable laughter that – to my alarm – the burly landlord came over to share the joke,

Quickly picking up my jacket, I beat a hasty retreat before the translation of 'gnat's piss' into Bulgarian could create a major diplomatic incident.

The music profession has a ceaseless knack of dishing out euphoric 'highs' one moment and terrible 'lows' the next. This happens with such startling regularity that it is often hard to know whether you are scaling a height, plumbing a depth or clutching vaguely at the limbo in between.

At 9.20 you could be in the middle of performing a Beethoven Sonata, in rapturous communion with one of the greatest minds of all time, yet by 9.45 you're jostling for a pint in the local boozer to the accompaniment not of a piano but a blaring juke-box.

More than once the effort to be sociable has proved too much for me. Apparently, when the organisers of the English Bach Festival took me off for a drink after my lunch-hour performance of two of the Bach Suites, they would have had every right to imagine I was under the influence of some potent extra-musical substance. But these works, despite being the earliest pieces of any real importance for the cello, remain at the very peak of its repertoire, and the glazed look in my eyes was caused not by the sight of the foaming glass placed before them but by music fit for the gods.

By then, of course, I should have been thoroughly used to these wild extremes of concert-life. The day after my student performance in front of the Queen Mother I was despatched by the College 'up North', along with pianist Simon Nicholls, to do a tour of comprehensive schools — it would be 'good experience'. Now, if northern clubs are a comedian's graveyard, at northern comprehensives a cellist is as good as six feet under before even drawing a bow.

Our first recital started well enough. The school's head — interrupted by occasional sniggers — gave a fulsome speech to the massed ranks of pupils:

'. . . What an honour and a privilege it is to be receiving a visit from two such brilliant young musicians who have come all the way from London to play for us. I am quite sure it will be a most memorable occasion which none of us, including the artists themselves, will ever forget.'

So far, so good, I thought, although becoming mildly alarmed by the flurry of titters which greeted the sight of my cello as I removed it from its case. I sat down and rested the instrument across my knees.

More titters.

And with breath that was by now thoroughly baited, pulled out the spike with a flourish.

Spasms of laughter.

My heart sank, but all was not lost — the first piece would show 'em. As a dramatic opener we had chosen Beethoven's G minor Sonata — a piece renowned for its explosive *fortissimos*.

It was a fatal mistake. Our first Beethovenian crash brought the house down, along with the loud pedal on Simon's upright.

Fresh gales of laughter, followed by a burst of applause, were all I needed to convince me that any further attempts to convert this rabble to Beethoven would be more than I and, more importantly, the piano could stand.

Surveying the sea of blank faces, I decided to try proceeding more on the lines of a 'lecture recital':

'Does anyone have any questions about playing the cello?' I ventured gingerly.

'Yea,' piped up a spotty boy from the back. 'Can you play Colonel Bogey?'

'What football team do you support?' shouted another, amid scenes of mounting chaos.

50

'Orient!' I snapped.

'Rubbish!' yelled most of the pupils — by this time in turmoil. The headmaster rose in a misguided attempt to retrieve the situation.

'I'm quite sure,' he boomed, 'that you could think of some much more sensible questions to ask Mr Lloyd Webber.'

For brief seconds silence reigned, despite the nudgings and winkings now running rife in the front row. From the middle of this new disturbance a well-upholstered young girl raised her hand.

'Yes?' I said, dreading her response with unknowing good reason.

'I've got a question for the keyboards man,' she giggled. 'Why is pianist sometimes pronounced peeeni. . . .'

Whatever she had in mind was drowned by the ensuing bedlam, and with law and order having irretrievably broken down we moved on, with sighs of relief, to the next 'school', having decided *that* one was not so much the pits of music-making as a veritable black hole.

Trouble also marred my New York début. With my programme of Debussy, Britten and Rachmaninov Sonatas complete, I played Rachmaninov's beautiful slow movement again as an encore.

After spending the previous two hours in an attempt to scale the heights, I left the platform in something of a trance but with the strangest feeling that something had been 'going on' during the encore.

It had.

'How on *earth* did you keep calm through all that!' exclaimed the first bejewelled lady to clasp my hand. 'It must have been *so* distracting.'

Gradually, the story unfolded. During the encore a street gang had broken into the prestigious Lincoln Center Hall, run the length of the gangway and forced their way out the other side — terrorising even this battle-hardened Manhattan audience. Fortunately, the glories of Rachmaninov's music had cushioned me from this slice of New York street-life taking place only yards from the platform.

51

A whole network of music clubs exists in Britain run entirely by enthusiastic amateurs. It is an astonishing system much envied abroad, as not only do these clubs attract professional musicians to parts of the country which would otherwise never hear a live concert, but they also provide invaluable experience for young soloists.

I remember the American impresario Harold Shaw telling me that he wished there was a similar network of organisations in the States, because — apart from the University circuit — there is nowhere for a young soloist to gain concert experience and perfect his art.

Although young musicians are the lifeblood of these clubs, quite a few have played host to some of the greatest names in music — even though they are often forced into using the local school gym or assembly hall for their concerts.

One of my first professional engagements was at a woefully decrepit old Town Hall in the North of England. As I stood on the platform surveying the decaying auditorium, the club organiser appeared by my side. He had a misty look in his eyes.

'Oh yes,' he sighed, 'we've had all the great names here — everyone. Even Casals.'

Astonished at the thought that the maestro might have stood on this very spot, I asked, unthinkingly, how he had played. The reply was truly northern.

'Not impressed, really. We thought he was having an off day.'

Without the amazing and, at times, positively eccentric characters one meets along the way, concert-giving would not be nearly so eye-opening.

Another trip north took Simon Nicholls and myself to the aptly-named town of Old Goole. We arrived at this windswept outpost on a dismal November Saturday at the awful hour of 5.00 and began the usual sole-destroying search for a cup of tea and a bite to eat — simple reliefs which are invariably beyond most British towns during that dreadful void between the shops shutting and the pubs

52

opening. Not only that, there appeared to be a curfew. No-one was about except one old man, who was wandering around the street chuckling and gibbering to himself. In desperation, we asked him if he knew of any café which might still be open.

'So you want a cup of tea, do you?' he said accusingly. 'Well, just you two come with me,' at which he shambled off down the street, followed nervously by the two of us.

The 'café' certainly seemed a long way off and, as we traipsed behind, he began to question us – giggling and hugging himself all the while. No sooner had I gingerly mentioned that we had come up from London to give a concert than he stopped dead, staring about him wildly.

'You mean to say,' he gasped incredulously, 'that you've come all the way to Old Goole just to give a concert? And you're going to drive all the way back again tonight?'

As the truth sank in, he broke down completely and, howling and cackling, sank to the pavement – the tears rolling down his cheeks.

Pondering anew on the wisdom of our chosen profession, we slunk back to the car, tormented by the sound of his terrible laughter.

Once again the 'highs' and 'lows' of concert life were dramatically evident the night I met Jacqueline du Pré, following a gala performance at Sadlers Wells in aid of her fund for research into multiple sclerosis. Jackie was at the height of her powers when she was so tragically crippled by multiple sclerosis and meeting her, just after playing myself, made me feel profoundly grateful for my own good health.

Tragedy was also in evidence at another gala evening I took part in at Longleat – the magnificent ancestral home of Lord Bath. After my recital in aid of the New Hall Hospital, a cabaret was held in a huge marquee specially constructed beside the lake. Derek Nimmo – who was master of ceremonies for the evening – made everyone laugh with his remark that the only record he'd ever made had sat in the shops so long that the hole in the middle healed up. And I enjoyed a spirited discussion about modern music with Princess Margaret and Norman St John-Stevas, who was then Minister for the Arts.

When I left Longleat in the early hours, the party was still in full swing. The next morning I received several mystifying phone calls from the Press, who were asking all kinds of questions about the evening. I had no idea why they were so interested and simply concluded it was because royalty had attended.

Next day's papers provided the reason. Lord Bath's son, whom I had seen only a few hours before, had hanged himself shortly after the party.

'Gala' charity concerts are often prone to disaster, which is probably due to the large number of temperamental artists who are suddenly thrown together, most of whom are perfectionists and all of whom want more than their fair share of the invariably limited rehearsal time.

The entire cast — and indeed the theatre itself — had a narrow escape halfway through a charity gala in aid of the organisation KIDS, at Her Majesty's Theatre in London. The gala featured a vast array of ballet dancers including my dressing-room companion, Peter Schaufuss.

Thankfully — for these evenings are almost always too long — my solos were near the beginning and all I had to do was play a couple of short pieces. It was just as well they were short. As I left the stage, a fearful smell of burning was wafting its way down the corridor from the direction of our dressing-room. Cello-in-hand I rushed to the door and kicked it open. It was all too easy to see what had happened. Flames were leaping from the foot of the curtains and a charred, steaming pair of ballet tights lay in shreds beneath them. Obviously Peter had got bored waiting for his turn and had gone off for a stroll — forgetting that his tights were warming up on the radiator.

Having first made sure that my cello was safe, I battled with the blaze and attempted — in vain — to get rid of the overpowering stench of burnt hosiery.

Ten minutes later Peter reappeared — totally unmoved either by the smell or the sight of his devastated tights — and I left the theatre wondering whether this sort of thing was an everyday occurrence in the ballet world.

Every so often the accidents that plague these events work greatly in your favour. In 1981, BBC Radio 2 held a special gala evening called *A Century of Song* at the Royal Albert Hall. All manner of stars from the world of light entertainment were on the bill — from Dame Vera Lynn to Bucks Fizz — yet, as I was the only classical musician, I began to wonder whether my item would seem too serious. Providence prevailed. With a thunderous clanking, the spike fell out of the cello on the very last note of my piece. The applause was rapturous and the timing so superb that everyone assumed it was part of a new routine to lighten my act for Radio 2. Sadly, I'll never be able to repeat it.

With its enormous casts, the Royal Variety Performance is a sure source of pandemonium and backstage the scene is unbelievable. The year I performed there were even more artists than usual, as the show included a lengthy item on '25 Years of British Pop', which featured virtually everybody from Cliff Richard and the Shadows to Adam Ant.

Since I was playing the final variation from *Variations* my cello needed to be amplified — along with the rest of the group. So a special pick-up and lead were attached to the cello's bridge. All I would have to do was walk on stage and plug the lead into the input socket which had been cunningly attached to a very regal-looking gold chair. If only life were so simple!

Somehow, during the backstage mêlée, the chair disappeared. Panic ensued as the stagehands scoured the wings. Now there were only seconds before I was due to go on and still it was nowhere to be seen. By some miracle, the very moment my name was announced, the chair was thrust into my hand. But, of course, it should have already been out on stage. There was nothing for it. Clutching my cello and bow in one hand and the chair in the other, I swept onto the platform — wondering if the Queen was assuming that I always carried a gold chair with a specially fitted jack-plug wherever I went.

The advertising for these galas can be as precarious as the concerts themselves. One December I played for an organisation called 'Crisis at Christmas', which gives special help to down-and-outs during that season of goodwill. Mine momentarily evaporated when I caught sight of the huge poster outside the hall proclaiming:

'Crisis at Christmas — Julian Lloyd Webber in concert.'

Nevertheless, I do have many happy memories of charity concerts and I found one — at Snape Maltings, in the presence of the Queen Mother — particularly moving. Although it was one of those rather unnerving occasions when all the artists remain on stage and watch the others take their turn, it gave me a wonderful opportunity of hearing Sir Peter Pears and the harpist Osian Ellis, sing and play a piece which Benjamin Britten had written especially for them.

Sitting on a sofa just a few feet away, I will never forget the ringing resonance of Osian's harp. It can truly be said to have reached the parts that other harps cannot reach.

One of the biggest joys of my career has been the opportunity it has given me to introduce British music abroad where, quite often, it remains surprisingly little known.

I discovered this unwelcome truth on one of my first orchestral dates outside Britain when I played the Elgar Concerto with l'Orchestre de Radio-Télévision Luxembourg — apparently it was the Concerto's first broadcast performance in Luxembourg. Afterwards, the orchestra threw a party for all the local musical dignitaries, and it wasn't long before I was approached by a gushing middle-aged lady.

'You are from England, is that right?' she began. 'Now tell me, where is this Elgar from?'

That, together with the German radio producer who declared: 'No good music has been composed in Britain between Purcell (died 1695) and Britten (born 1913),' left me with no illusions as to the state of British music abroad. It was this ignorance of our musical heritage, rather than any nationalistic sense of pride, that determined me to include British music whenever possible on my foreign travels.

I suspect the neglect of British music abroad is partly due to the uncomfortable fact that the British instrumentalist has been a rare bird — if not an almost unknown species —

outside British waters until comparatively recently. This means that much of our finest music has hardly ever been heard abroad. There is no tradition, either of its performance or — equally important — of how it should be performed. The subtle nuances which are the very essence of a composer like Delius are virtually impossible to convey on paper and, in the absence of any authentic guidelines, such lyrical outpourings will mean little to the uninitiated musician sight-reading these pieces for the first time.

Often I find that foreign audiences are amazed by the quality of British compositions. In 1979 I introduced the John Ireland *Sonata* to Brazil — fifty-five years after it was published. I placed it at the end of the first half of my programme following Debussy's *Sonata*, an acknowledged masterpiece. On paper at least, the Ireland might have appeared a poor companion for such a fine work but the audiences — most of whom had never heard of John Ireland — were entranced by its spell — some even preferring it to the Debussy.

Even in Britain we underestimate our composers. For example, the Cello Sonatas by Delius, Ireland and Britten are among the best in the repertoire, yet how often do you hear them in live performance? And quite apart from the Elgar Concerto, there are many other fine works for cello and orchestra by composers such as Britten, Bridge, Delius, Holst, Moeran and Walton.

British music has always figured largely in my repertoire and, as well as the Elgar, the Delius Concerto is also very special to me. Frederick Delius composed some of the loveliest music ever written for the cello — music which, above all else, lets the instrument sing. I have recorded all of his cello music, right from the very early *Romance* — written in the days when he called himself Fritz Delius — to the *Sonata*, the *Concerto* and finally the late *Caprice and Elegy* which the then blind and paralysed composer dictated to a young Yorkshireman named Eric Fenby with whom, years later, I was to play the Sonata in public.

Working so closely with Eric was a truly awe-inspiring

59

experience — almost uncannily like communicating with Delius himself some fifty years after his death. Our recording of the Sonata was actually made using Delius's own piano — played, of course, by the very man who had been 'the composer's eyes and hands', as Eric later recalled.

If I had to single out just one of Delius's works for cello it would have to be the Concerto. This rapturous piece, with its abundance of beautiful melodies and ravishing orchestral textures, is a luscious paradise garden of cello sound. Nevertheless, when the BBC asked me to make my Prom début with the Concerto, I was more than a little worried. Because the piece was so rarely played, I knew that many of the audience would be hearing it for the first time and wondered if Delius's timeless musings might be lost in the vast spaces of the Albert Hall.

The atmosphere of the Proms is quite unique, with the promenaders pressed right up against a barrier in front of the platform — almost like the crowd at a football match, and I began to wonder whether the youthful audience would become restless during such an intimate piece.

My fears could not have proved more unfounded for I have rarely known a more rapt and attentive audience. It was a moment to treasure.

British composers have been strongly drawn to the cello, finding in it a restrained and melancholy nobility. Benjamin Britten, who wrote five major cello works, is a composer whose spirit pervades the places where he lived and worked. The countryside surrounding Aldeburgh — flat and desolate, yet strangely beautiful — was so much a part of his work that it is impossible not to feel his presence in his Snape Maltings Concert Hall, home of the Aldeburgh Festival.

To me the sound of the cello has a quite natural connection with the countryside, and no composer could have been more profoundly influenced by England's rolling landscape than Edward Elgar. Elgar's spirit was truly a part of the Malvern Hills he knew and loved so dearly. As he lay dying, he clasped the hand of his great friend, the violinist William Reed, and started to hum the lilting 9/8 theme from the first movement of his Cello Concerto.

'Willy,' he said with tears in his eyes, 'if you're out walking on the Malverns and you hear that music, don't worry — it will only be me.'

The cello has a natural sound — a voice of nature — and Elgar's music belongs to such an instrument.

The cello's link with nature became notorious through that much underrated cellist Beatrice Harrison (who was soloist on Elgar's own recording of his Cello Concerto). By the 1920s and '30s the nightingale had become a rare bird in Britain but Miss Harrison found that the sound of her cello drifting through the open windows had enticed a nightingale back to her Surrey garden. On hearing the news, the BBC immediately despatched a team of radio engineers down to Surrey. It would be the BBC's first ever outside broadcast. With microphones at the ready Miss Harrison began to play. At first the bird was silent, but gradually the sound of the music prompted its voice and the song of the nightingale, accompanied by Beatrice's cello, was broadcast all over the world.

Sadly it is for this, rather than her revelatory interpretations, that Beatrice Harrison is chiefly remembered — a clear warning to any cellist who might be thinking of straying beyond the boundaries of convention.

A performance may be directly affected by the concert hall itself. Most musicians, especially string players, prefer an acoustic which allows the instrument to sing — in other words, a hall with resonance. A 'dry' hall means more vibrato, more emphasis on projection and, in general, a much harder evening's work.

Some halls have a marvellous sound when empty but are disappointing when full, and vice versa. More often than not, the best acoustics are the result of pure chance and they can sometimes be found in the most unexpected places. Who would think, for example, that the Assembly Rooms in Walthamstow and the Town Hall in Watford are two of the most sought-after venues for orchestral recording in the world?

A hall's atmosphere can also have a great effect on the performer and a very few halls have such a magic combination of atmosphere and acoustics that they actually help to 'lift' the performance. Among these charmed buildings I would certainly include Edinburgh's wonderful Usher Hall, the Maltings at Snape, the modern 'Konserthuset' in Gothenburg and the Philharmonie in Berlin. Another inspirational place to play is Helsinki's Temppeliaukio Church — which is often used during their Summer Festival. Literally hewn out of the rock, it has the sort of atmosphere so often looked for, but so rarely found, in a modern concert hall.

On stage, the Albert Hall is surprisingly friendly and intimate. It is so vast and the audience seems so far away that
the platform feels like a little world on its own and you can
almost imagine you're playing at home in your living room.

A curious substitute for the concert hall is provided by
theatres. Not only is the scenery for whatever play happens
to be running often left on stage, so that one's Beethoven
Sonata appears to be taking place in a Persian market, but
the wings are a pitch-black minefield of wires and ropes — a
myriad of all kinds of props — anything, in fact, that could
conceivably cause a cellist with a protruding spike to fall
flat on his face. However, in the safety of the dressing-room,
entertainment of a sort is often provided by the theatre's
tannoy system, which relays not only your 'calls' but
sometimes a snatch of audience conversation as well.
During one interval my efforts to relax were interrupted by
an extraordinarily heated discussion between two gentle-
men on the question of whether or not I had recorded the
Bax Concerto. (I hadn't and haven't.) Unable to turn the
disturbance off, I was sorely tempted to go out front and
settle the argument there and then — at least it would have
given me a bit of peace backstage!

Apart from acoustics and atmosphere, it is surprising what
mundane things contribute to a successful concert. Like
chairs, for example. Chairs are the cellists' fetish — they
must not have arms, must not squeak and must definitely
not be too comfortable — in other words, the ideal seat for a
cellist is a good old kitchen chair.

Hall managers disagree, and invariably I will arrive for
my rehearsal to find a fabulously sumptuous specimen
waiting for me on the platform. It will have splendid
carvings and plush, velvety cushions and will be disdain-
fully cast aside, to be replaced by the dusty plastic chair
which I've unearthed from the broom cupboard. The
height of the chair is also crucial, for if it is too low or too
high, the angle of your body to the instrument is all wrong
and you can spend the entire concert feeling shifty.

So chairs are an understandable source of neurosis for

cellists, and there was a time when — on special occasions — I used to take our kitchen chair along as well. But matters came to a head one baking hot day when I insisted on bringing it all the way from London to Bristol in the Mini. While I did the driving, the cello had pride of place beside me, and Celia, the pianist, a friend of his *and* the chair were all forced to take a back seat. In the end I decided that the childish displays of temper shown by my various passengers were more trouble than even my magnificent chair was worth.

Like chairs, the rostrum which cellists sit on during concerts can begin to achieve a significance out of all proportion to its unimposing appearance. As this wooden box raises the cellist a good nine inches from the stage, many people think it is put there merely to enable the audience to see him better, but the rostrum is really intended to help the cello project its sound into the hall by acting as a sort of sounding board. Unfortunately, some are much too narrow which means your feet dangle precariously over the edges, while others are so high that, peering down from the platform, you are gripped by a sudden attack of vertigo.

It is small wonder that most orchestras have become so used to the foibles of cellists that they now solemnly cart an appointed chair and rostrum from place to place wherever they go.

Phobias about chairs and rostrums are common to all cellists, but soloists will have a few extra eccentricities of their own. I can never understand why Celia looks so distraught when I systematically cut off the sleeves just above the elbow every time I buy an expensive new dress shirt as — no longer burdened by these — I can then dispense with the tedium of having to remember cuff links and also feel greater freedom of movement during concerts.

Another, altogether unhealthier, peculiarity is my obsession that my left hand fingers should never be touched by water. This is because the softening effect of water on the fingertips makes the cello strings feel rough and cutting. This cat-like insistence on avoiding water has caused some considerable embarrassments — like the time I was forced into a swimming pool in Brazil and, using one hand, could only manage to swim round and round in circles! But at least it provided me with a perfect excuse for not doing the washing-up — until Celia bought me a pair of rubber gloves for Christmas!

I suppose it is possible that this mildly disgusting habit could have led to the poisoned finger which, back in January 1973, nearly caused the cancellation of my first ever performance of the Delius Concerto. This was a live broadcast from Manchester Town Hall, and even with my delvings into obscure performances on foreign radio stations it appeared to be the concerto's first live performance in years. But, after practising the intricate solo part for weeks, I developed a poisoned third finger the night before the first rehearsal. Helped by massive doses of penicillin I struggled through the rehearsal, but the more I played the more the finger throbbed and next day's broadcast began to seem an impossibility.

To make matters worse I had attempted to save money by booking in at a dismal hotel somewhere round the back of Victoria Station — which must have been the coldest, shabbiest, most broken-down in the city and which has thankfully (in case anybody else is thinking of spending a cheap night in Manchester) long since been pulled down. Even if I had been able to practise, there wasn't enough space in my room to draw a bow across the strings, and the fact that I never seemed to have enough 5p's for the meter on the electric fire only added to the misery of that bitterly cold January evening.

That night I lay in bed, seriously wondering whether the idea of being a solo cellist was not a big mistake. Here I was, after practising hard on a concerto I had wanted to play for years, lying in this freezing, miserable, little hotel room, almost certain to have to cancel the next day's concert. Not only that, the performance was billed in the *Radio Times* and it seemed terrible to be letting down listeners who — for all I knew — had been hoping to hear a live performance of the Delius for years. It was this overriding thought that sent me to sleep in fighting mood. I would get through that concert somehow.

If, on that black night, I wondered for a moment whether I had chosen the right profession, I was given the answer in 1976. For that summer, it seemed as if everything I had worked towards since I was thirteen was about to be taken away from me, and I would never be able to play the cello again. The fact that I still can is due to a Mrs Brown.

Ever since I began playing the cello I would occasionally feel a stab of pain — like the jab of a needle through a nerve — deep inside the first finger of my left hand. The pain would be so bad that my hand would instinctively leap from the string but, just as quickly, it would vanish and I would continue with my practice and think nothing more of it. That summer, everything changed.

One morning I was playing, rather ironically, a quiet, contemplative piece by my father. Suddenly, the pain struck. My finger flew off the string, but this time as soon as I put it back, the pain seared again.

Now I was seriously worried. It could have been in the middle of a concert. Nervously, I took myself off to the doctor. He could find no sign of any problem and, with a sigh of relief, I returned to my practice. A few days later, the pain struck again. This time I went to see a hand specialist. He could also find no sign of any external problem and an X-ray was arranged to determine whether anything had worked its way underneath the surface of the skin. This revealed nothing, and the general medical opinion seemed to be that the finger must have been overworked and perhaps I should try a course of ultrasonic treatment. Reluctantly, I agreed.

Every day I went for the treatments, but still the pains persisted. In desperation I was sent to a skin specialist and given a special cream which was designed to remove the layers of skin — just in case something might be lying way beneath, undetected. All the while I continued giving concerts, well aware that news of the problem could not be allowed to spread. For the implications were all too plain to see — at twenty-five, my playing days looked as if they were over.

66

That August, one of my fondest ambitions was to be fulfilled. I had been invited to play the Elgar Concerto at the Three Choirs Festival, that historical festival where Elgar had conducted so many moving performances of his own works. The concert would be in the Cathedral at Hereford — that wonderful setting where England meets with Wales and where Elgar's spirit belongs.

By the week of the concert the pains had become so continuous I was convinced it would be my last performance. The fact that it was not is the result of an experience which is hard to explain.

A little while before the Three Choirs concert, my mother had been introduced to Mrs Rosemary Brown — the lady who created a sensation with her claim that she was receiving music from dead composers. Mrs Brown had mentioned that she also practised spiritual healing, and the doctors' admission that there was nothing further they could do for me jogged my mother's memory. In my present state it seemed that *anything* would be worth a try and with the negative thought that nothing, now, could do my finger any further damage, I rang Mrs Brown. She asked to see me that very evening.

As Celia drove me to Mrs Brown's house I had the hopeless feeling that I was clutching at straws. Would it not be better to admit to myself that my career was over?

It was with these thoughts that we found our way to the little terraced house in South London. Mrs Brown came to the door and showed us to her front room. After a few minutes she took hold of my hand. Slowly, very gently, she began to rub the tip of my first finger and a feeling of heat began to grow inside to the point where I wondered whether she might trigger off the pain.

At last she finished, and we sat together in hushed silence.

Mrs Brown spoke first:

'I think you should rub a little warm olive oil into the fingertip every day,' she said in a matter-of-fact way. 'That will help to keep it supple and it won't give you any further trouble.'

I didn't believe her. But over the next few weeks — as

67

each new day went by free from pain — my confidence began to grow, and since that remarkable evening, more than eight years ago, the pain has never returned.

That summer was a turning point in my life. Up until then I had occasionally doubted whether I really wanted the life of a solo musician, with all its struggles and uncertainties, but, faced with the thought of a life without my constant friend and companion, I knew I would have given everything I had to play the cello again.

There is no doubt that the music profession can be pretty cut-throat at times. An example concerns my relationship, or rather lack of relationship, with the Halle Orchestra. I gave my one and only concert with them playing the Elgar Concerto at the Halle Proms conducted by Vernon Handley. I remember the day well — it was 14 July 1976, five days after the troubles began with my finger. On the 10th I gave a recital and the day before the Halle concert I broadcast Strauss's *Don Quixote* with Manchester's other orchestra — the BBC Northern. Amazingly, both dates went very well but by the evening of the 13th the toll was really beginning to tell and, for the second time in four years in Manchester, I found myself wondering whether it would be possible to go ahead with next day's concert. The problem was that in order to avoid playing on the painful part of the finger I had to alter completely the hand position I'd used since I first began playing. This was bad enough in the middle of important concerts, but worse was the fact I was now putting tremendous pressure on a part of the finger never used before which had become, as a result, extremely sore.

Few people can realise the amount of pressure applied to the fingertips during a concert. Imagine placing them on a taut metal wire and then putting the full weight of your arm behind them and you will understand what I mean.

Obviously, with lots of practice, your fingertips become hard and tough — oblivious to this kind of pressure and you forget just how much you are asking from them. If they get a bit sore it is no good thinking: 'I'll take it easy today and use a little less pressure', as the pressure is so great that 'a little less' would make no difference and because, in every concert and even in rehearsals, you must give everything.

So I was in a pretty bad way when I took the platform of the Free Trade Hall that night. I love the Elgar and really wanted to do it justice, but psychologically the performance must have been handicapped by my knowledge that, if I touched the nerve in my finger, the concert would have to stop.

Despite my worries the Concerto was well received and a large number of the orchestra, including the cello section, came to my room to say they had enjoyed it. Although I had to travel back to London that night to rehearse for a recording of Ireland's Piano Trios, I agreed with Clive Smart, the manager of the orchestra, to stay through the second half (I was finished by the interval) and attend a reception being given by the sponsors of the concert — 'it would mean so much to the orchestra'.

However, it was not long before word came back through my agents that the Halle management had not been too impressed with my playing and over the next few years, when my name was mentioned as a possible soloist to them, nothing materialised.

Early in 1981, however, the inexpensive Classics for Pleasure label decided that they wanted to continue their excellent series of recordings with the conductor Vernon Handley and make a record of Delius's orchestral music — including the Cello Concerto. This was an idea which greatly appealed to me, as the Concerto is unfairly neglected and would have reached a far larger public than usual on a low-priced recording. Simon Foster, the manager of Classics for Pleasure and one of the nicest people I have met in the record business, wanted to use me as soloist with the Halle Orchestra (which apparently had some kind of deal with CfP).

I told Simon he would have to move fast, because I was

close to signing an exclusive contract with another record company who would doubtless refuse to allow me to record for CfP. The Halle were on tour in the Far East at the time so Clive Smart was telexed for his answer. Simon received the rather strange reply that the Cello Concerto was 'not Halle repertoire'*, but that other music by Delius was always of interest. However, said Smart, if we might perhaps find 'an independent backer' for the Cello Concerto then it could be reconsidered! In other words, money talks. Although this was roughly what I had expected, Simon was astonished by Smart's decision and so we approached the Delius Trust — who have sponsored many fine Delius recordings — to see if they would consider contributing towards it. All the while valuable time was being lost and I stressed to Simon it would not be long before I was unable to make the recording anyway.

Within a few months, after a lot of hard work from both of us, the Trust agreed to cover the costs of recording the Concerto. Would the Halle agree this time? Amazingly they did, and two live concerts were even 'pencilled in' at Buxton and Chester — suddenly the Concerto was Halle repertoire! What seemed odd, however, was that contracts for these mid-September dates were singularly unforthcoming and had still not appeared by July (contracts are often signed well over a year in advance).

Then what had looked increasingly likely happened. RCA offered me an exclusive contract. I went to see Don Ellis, head of RCA UK and, as expected, he said it would be out of the question for me to proceed with recording a piece that I was strongly associated with for CfP (I had made my Prom début with the Delius the previous year) when just about to sign for RCA.

The news that I could no longer record the Delius for CfP was broken to both Simon Foster and the Halle immediately. Simon was wonderful about the whole thing and wrote a sweet letter congratulating me on the RCA contract. Were the Halle so pleased? Not quite. Apparently

* Sir John Barbirolli had conducted the Halle in the Concerto with the orchestra's own principal cellist as soloist.

the concert at Buxton was now 'definite', and had even been advertised. Quite why the concert at Chester wasn't suddenly 'definite' as well, I never discovered but – unknown to me – the Halle issued a statement saying I was 'unable to prepare the concerto in time' for the concert at Buxton – which must have seemed a little odd to anyone who had been at my Huddersfield performance of the work a few months before.

To this day the Halle remains the only professional orchestra in Britain I have played with and not returned to and I have to admit to feeling just a touch of extra pleasure when my recording of the Delius Concerto finally appeared on RCA with the same excellent conductor, Vernon Handley, but a different orchestra – the Philharmonia.

One thing a young artist needs is a good agent. I was fortunate to be invited to join Ibbs & Tillett at the beginning of my career, but it is not always easy for an aspiring soloist to find the right agent. Should he, for example, opt for the large agency – with its huge list of artists and limitless contacts – or should he choose a smaller management that might have fewer connections but work harder for its artists? It's an age-old problem, but whichever alternative is chosen he will find most classical agents are fundamentally honest, at least in my experience. There are rarely vast sums of money to be made in classical music management and many agents work long and hard for precious little reward.

Every so often the odd bit of sharp practice does come to light, and one early victim was none other than Pablo Casals. Halfway through his first American tour, Casals discovered that his New York agent was charging the promoters considerably more than he had been led to believe and was simply pocketing the difference. This amounted to several hundred dollars a concert which, in those days, was a lot of money. Rather than say anything immediately, he continued to watch the situation. When the tour was over, he invited his manager to meet him at his hotel with the promise that the conversation would not take up much time. The meeting arranged, Casals began his plan of campaign. Placing two chairs near the hotel entrance, he ushered the man to the seat nearest the door. After a few pleasantries the agent enquired how everything had gone.

'Fine,' replied Casals, 'apart from the fact that you've been robbing me.' Immediately the man rose, pale and flustered, and Casals leapt to action. Shoving him into the hotel's revolving doors, he began to spin them round as fast as he could until, suddenly, they broke. For a few seconds Casals watched his former agent hobbling off down the street before the hotel manager called him back to pay for the damage. Doubtless Casals was the first in the long line of musicians who have vandalised their hotels!

By and large musicians seem to have a love-hate relationship with their agents — it's love when the work is coming in and hate when it isn't. Perhaps their attitude is best summed up by the story of the pianist whose performance was interrupted by the unmistakable sound of a telephone ringing off-stage. Without missing a note he shouted to the wings:

'If that's my agent, tell him I'm working.'

Many people seem to think the classical music world would be above the sort of envies and backbiting that are notorious in other professions. The thought of an artist playing such beautiful music on the platform, while indulging in such petty behaviour off it, seems inconceivable to most concert-goers. Yet it would be less than honest if, among the pitfalls and pressures of the music business, rivalry amongst 'colleagues' was not even mentioned. Jealousies are probably inevitable when so many people are vying for position in such a highly specialised area, and people who have worked in both the theatre and classical music will tell you that the musical world fares just as high on the backbiting stakes!

A great insight into the profession was provided by no less a figure than the conductor Otto Klemperer. A friend of his was pointing out how many famous conductors had died during the course of that year. Lugubriously, he began to list their names.

'Ja, ja,' interrupted the irritable Klemperer. 'It's been a good year, hasn't it?'

What are the attributes needed for success in such a tough profession? Talent is just the starting point — there can be no chance of lasting success without it. Dedication, determination, stamina and, at times, the hide of a fairly stocky rhinoceros are other necessary qualities.

This last quality — if you can call it that — worries me. It implies insensitivity yet surely, to be able to convey deeply felt human emotions through music and to penetrate the often highly sensitive minds of its creators, a great degree of sensitivity is needed? Are we in danger of producing a tough new breed of robot-like musicians who jet round the world giving almost identical performances which are merely technically proficient?

Courage also plays an enormous part in the early stages of a career. Nowadays there are so many young musicians aiming for the heights that, to stand a chance, they must be prepared to take every opportunity to be heard — even at the risk of failure.

One of my earliest 'breaks' came as a result of taking a chance that seemed to involve the risk of failure on a massive scale! Soon after I joined Ibbs & Tillett they phoned me with a harrowing question.

'Do you know Richard Strauss's *Don Quixote*?'

I certainly knew it by repute — as one of the longest,

most complex pieces for cello and orchestra — but it was a complete blind spot. I had never even seen the music, let alone played it.

'Why, yes *of course*, I know it well,' I lied, knowing full well an engagement was in the offing. 'Why do you ask?'

'Because the soloist with the Royal Liverpool Philharmonic has fallen ill and they have to find a replacement immediately. Sir Charles Groves is conducting and will want to hear you play it before engaging you. When can you see him?'

In total panic I wondered whether to own up.

'When's the concert?' I stuttered.

'There are four — Liverpool, Wolverhampton, Edinburgh and Glasgow. The first is in ten days' time but, of course, Sir Charles will want to hear you as soon as possible. When can you take it to him?'

'Hold on, I'll check my diary.'

Thumbing through the pages my heart sank. I had four concerts between now and the one in Liverpool — there would hardly be any time to learn a piece I didn't know at all. On the other hand if I refused, they might never ask again. I took what seemed the biggest gamble of my life.

'Just give me three days to brush the piece up and then I'll play it to Sir Charles.'

Suddenly realising I did not even have the music, I rang the main London music shops to see if they had a copy. They had not. With mounting desperation I rang Douggie Cameron — surely *he* would have one? Quickly I explained my problem.

'You'll never manage *Don Quixote* in that time,' he drawled 'but you're welcome to come and get my copy if you like.'

That night, unable to sleep, I lay in bed haunted by Cameron's words, wondering if I'd made a terrible mistake. Finally drifting off, I woke in a cold sweat with a vision of being on a platform in front of thousands of people with no idea what I was supposed to be playing (a recurrent musicians' nightmare!).

For the next three days, and most of the nights, I spent every available moment on the Strauss. When I wasn't

76

practising, I was listening to it on record and by the time Sir Charles opened the door of his flat it was Don Quixote who stepped into his sitting-room rather than Julian Lloyd Webber. Pronouncing himself satisfied, Sir Charles confirmed the engagements. I continued to practise furiously and, in the end, even managed to play the piece from memory.

With the tour over, my delight was completed by Sir Charles's announcement that he was so pleased that he had decided to repeat *Don Quixote* at the orchestra's Royal Festival Hall concert in three months' time.

Opportunities like this may not be too good for the nervous system but they must be taken. Not long afterwards I shared the platform in Hamburg with a highly talented young pianist who had defected from Russia. She seemed in a dreadful flap because she'd been invited to play the Tchaikovsky Concerto in the Royal Albert Hall at 'short notice'. Thinking she only had a few days to learn it, I asked when the performance was.

'Only three months' time,' she said hopelessly. 'How can I learn the Tchaikovsky in three months?'

Cruel as it may seem I came to the conclusion that this girl would never make it. Few soloists can concentrate on one piece of music for that length of time, to the exclusion of all else.

Another vital thing I learned from the start was that you must give your best on every occasion, no matter what the conditions. On one of my first tours I gave five performances of the Elgar Concerto in quick succession with the Bournemouth Symphony Orchestra. One of these was a Radio 3 broadcast the morning after our third concert which had been at Plymouth before a large and appreciative audience. After the intensity of the performance, a late night and the drive back to Bournemouth, the last thing I felt like, on waking to a particularly dismal morning, was playing the Concerto all over again to nothing but a microphone.

Some eight months later I opened the *Radio Times* to discover the broadcast was not only going out at peak time in the evening on both Radios 3 and 4, but had also been given star billing, complete with my photo and extracts from reviews of my previous Elgar performances. Suddenly everyone was phoning up, promising to tune in — it seemed all the world would be listening. Remembering little of the broadcast, I began to panic. Maybe the performance had been as dismal as the Bournemouth morning?

That evening I sat tensely by the radio, but by the end of the first movement I felt more relaxed — there had been no slipping of standards. Indeed, the performance was heard by Sir Georg Solti who later invited me to perform the Concerto with him at the Royal Festival Hall.

Dedication may seem an obvious prerequisite for success, but it would certainly be as well for any aspiring soloist to know just how all-consuming a vocation it can be. For a start you are never really on holiday. Although it may seem easy for a musician to take time off, it is impossible to go for days without practice and then expect to play just as well as ever.

If I am away from the cello for any length of time, I start feeling distinctly edgy. Even after a few days' holiday I will be itching to get back to work, but sometimes it seems the effort of dragging myself back to peak playing condition is so great that it was hardly worth taking the holiday in the first place. Each artist will have a different method for keeping his technique up to standard and, for me, this means at least four hours' practice every day — including Sundays.

The pianist Paderewski said it all:

'If I don't practise for one day *I* know it, if I don't practise for two days the *critics* know it and if I don't practise for three days the *audience* knows it.'

Music is a hard task-master, and it is essential that those around you understand how all-absorbing it can be. Hopefully my own personal nadir of self-absorption was reached on my wedding day, which happened to be the day after I had given a Festival Hall concert. As Celia reached the altar, her worst doubts about the wisdom of marrying me must have been confirmed by my whispered:

'Have you seen the reviews yet?'

If a sense of humour is essential for the people close to a soloist, it is just as vital a requirement for the soloist himself. One day in 1976, after what had seemed like years of struggle, a contract dropped through the letter-box which at last realised all my dreams. Unable to contain my excitement, I yelled down the corridor to my wife.

'Celia! I don't believe it! I've got a date at Carnegie Hall!'

Celia rushed into the room and flung her arms around me but my eyes had already caught sight of the all-important small print at the foot of the contract. It read:

'CARNEGIE HALL, Workington.'

With all the travelling involved, stamina and health are obvious essentials for a soloist. You need to be able to drive home after a concert, yet still have the energy to get up and practise a different concerto early next morning. Some soloists have an almost legendary capacity for hard living. Rostropovich, for example, seems to be able to go without sleep for days, yet even he has sometimes fallen victim to punishing schedules. Apparently, at a performance in Turin, he dozed off during the long orchestral introduction of Dvořák's Concerto. Awoken too late by the key change which heralds the soloist's entry, a startled Rostropovich had no alternative but to call a halt to the proceedings. Turning to the conductor he whispered:

'You played so magnificently I was spellbound. Please play it again.'

It is not always easy to catch enough sleep on tour. Apart from all the strange hotel rooms, there was a time when I couldn't sleep for worrying about the next day's performance. Nowadays, I find it hard to sleep *afterwards* as I relive the performance over and over again in my mind.

Often the hotel delivers a rude awakening. Padding bleary-eyed around your adopted bedroom, you suddenly catch sight of a fearsome intruder creeping under the door.

It is the morning paper with its review of last night's concert.

Now many an artist will tell you they do not read their reviews, but do you really believe that alone in their hotel rooms, they don't cast a sneaky glance at the unmentionable?

Although a strong stomach is sometimes needed to digest the critics' prognostications, I tend to go along with the view of one of my favourite authors, Arthur Machen. Machen actually collected together some of his worst reviews (along with a handful of good ones) and published them in a volume called *Precious Balms*. In a very interesting introduction he explains his belief that there is nothing so boring as continuous praise:

'Opposition, whether it be that of a mountain side or a body of critical opinion, is one of the chiefest zests and relishes of life.'

Most critics take their work very seriously, although there will always be the few who feel they are not doing their job properly unless they engage in an act of destruction. Some, however, do not know their job at all.

Following a performance of Rachmaninov's Sonata at Snape Maltings, I played the Slow Movement again as an encore. I could hardly believe it when the editor of a well-known British music magazine came up to me afterwards and asked what the encore had been, even though he had heard the same movement only ten minutes before.

Countless stories have been told which show critics in a bad light but perhaps it is easy to forget just how much music they do have to listen to. Years ago a critic on *The Observer* suffered a serious 'memory lapse'. He completely dismissed a new violin sonata by Eugene Goossens which, in his notice, he claimed to be hearing for the first time. Later it transpired that not only had he heard the same sonata played by the same artists a few months before, but had also given it a rave review.

On balance I think it is helpful to read the critics but it certainly doesn't do to take them too seriously. For example, what was to be made of the reviews of my recital for the Royal Dublin Society? According to the *Irish Times* I

81

had played superbly but the concert had been marred by the total inadequacy of my pianist. Yet in the *Irish Press* my disastrous performance had only been saved by my pianist's undoubted brilliance.

However, this pales in comparison to the critical dissent which followed the première of the Concerto which Rodrigo wrote for me. Depending on your Sunday paper, it was either 'a dismal little squib . . . a medley of jottings that drifts aimlessly from one point to the next' (*The Observer*), or 'Its attractive melodies, striking rhythms and instrumental coups were totally conquering. The rare encore demanded by the audience indicated the work's magic.' (*The Sunday Times*).

Perhaps my best ever set of reviews followed that emotional performance at the Three Choirs Festival I believed might be my last. It would certainly be nice to flatter myself that the performance had, indeed, been quite exceptional. But I remember only too well my horrendous discovery that it had been wholly unique for a different reason. I had played the entire concerto with my flies undone.

If the critics are sometimes puzzling, then their colleagues on other pages of the newspaper are equally baffling. I am constantly surprised by their idea of a 'good story'. Musical items rarely seem to fall into this category unless you are doing something you are 'not supposed to'. For example, a first performance in years of a forgotten\work by a major composer will be lucky to achieve a paragraph of editorial, but my concerts with Stephane Grappelli received massive coverage — likewise the *Variations* album. To me they are all of equal importance.

It is impossible to predict what topics the press will seize upon. For instance, I was surprised at their reaction to my agreeing to take a few pupils at the Guildhall School of Music — suddenly there were headlines proclaiming 'Cellist a professor at 26'. Then there was the bizarre episode of the 'Addict Cellist'.

Twice in my life I have experienced the unpleasant condition of having a stone in the kidney. The second time my doctor immediately diagnosed the problem.* There is little you can do once a stone has formed except wait for it to pass but, one night, the pain became so great that I was rushed to Westminster Hospital as an emergency patient. Even though my doctor had arranged for me to be admitted, and in spite of Celia's protests, the hospital doctor refused to believe I had a kidney stone. For three hours I was left literally writhing in agony despite all my pleas for a pain killer. Later the hospital admitted that they had thought 'anyone with a name like Lloyd Webber coming from an area like Kensington was probably an addict trying on an act to get drugs'. Celia reported the incident to the Patients' Association and, within days, it was splashed all over the papers with headlines like '*Cellist an addict?*' which cheered me up immensely.

What might have interested the press still further was the way my ailment was finally cured. One evening − after more than a week spent in agony, unable to eat and with no sign of the stone passing − Celia contacted Rosemary Brown. This time, I must confess, I was thoroughly sceptical. How on earth could she begin to tackle something as physical as a stone lodged in the kidney?

Rosemary arrived the same evening and I awoke to find her sitting quietly by my side. As she placed her hand on my kidney, she began to pray. A little while later she assured me that the stone was beginning to break up and would probably be gone by the morning. Suddenly the pain grew even more intense − the stone was already moving. Two hours later it had passed.

Anything to do with money interests the press enormously. When I bought my Stradivarius cello in auction at Sotheby's they latched on to it immediately, even though I had made my bid anonymously. Instantly it was assumed that I must be fabulously rich, and a few days later an article appeared

* For information on what happened the first time, please contact Colin Webb c/o Pavilion Books

in *The Sunday Times* mentioning that I had commissioned Rodrigo's Cello Concerto. This was right enough, but somehow along the line the commission fee quoted had grown to *twenty* times the true figure. A correction was printed the following week.

The Press are not the only ones prone to exaggeration. News of even a minor mishap travels fast in the music world. A couple of months later it will emerge, suitably embellished, as a major incident. Once, after a broadcast of the Schumann Concerto, I was asked by the BBC producer if I would be prepared to play the opening few bars again, as apparently there had been some interference on the tape. The audience remained patiently behind for the retake and eventually the producer was happy.

Six weeks later, after a recital at the Chichester Festival, the Festival Director asked me whether it was really true that I'd sworn so continuously at all my dreadful mistakes that the BBC had forced me to play the whole concerto again!

The prices paid for top instruments are certainly extraordinary. While still a student, I remember trying Jacqueline du Pré's Stradivarius cello (The Davidoff) and being shocked to hear it would fetch 'at least £30,000' on the open market. Thirteen years later the same instrument was reputed to be on sale for no less than $1,000,000 (approximately £700,000). The thought that what is basically just a piece of wood can be worth that sort of money may be unbelievable, but even though no instrument, however superb, can turn a mediocre player into a good one, many string players will save all their lives, making many sacrifices, to buy the instrument of their dreams.

What makes the difference between a good cello and a great one? In the first place, a cello needs great power and penetration to be able to project to the back of a vast concert hall, yet it is often those very qualities that cause the instrument to sound harsh and grating close to. A cello which truly combines power with real sweetness of tone is rare indeed. Add to that the indefinable genius of a craftsman like Stradivarius and you have prices to match.

However a great name will by no means guarantee a great instrument. Many fine instruments have been so over-restored that little of their original craftsmanship remains, and sometimes they have been tampered with to such an extent that they are now almost unplayable. For example quite a few early cellos were considered too big to play on comfortably and were consequently reduced in size. Later, fashion decreed they were now too small and they were extended again! It is hardly surprising when an instrument treated in this way develops problems.

In 1978 Edward Heath gave me the opportunity of borrowing a 'Strad'. The instrument had been left to him and, with great kindness, he invited me over to his home to try it out. Unfortunately, from the first few strokes of the bow I knew it was not the cello for me and, with what felt like great ingratitude, politely declined his offer. Later, I heard that the dealers had decided it was not a Strad after all.

It has almost become a cliché for a string player to say that his relationship with his instrument is like a marriage, but in many ways it is so very true. Hours a day are spent trying to tame this temperamental creature who means so much to you. The instrument is your companion at some of the most testing moments of your life — moments you have worked towards together — and it is hardly surprising that it should feel such a great rift to be parted from something you have shared so much with. When I was forced to sell my first good cello (to buy a supposedly better one), I freely admit to shedding a few tears on my way home from its new owner.

However, my perspective on the value of instruments was obviously not shared by a certain television cameraman. Immediately after forking out a vast sum for my eighteenth century Stradivarius we did a television programme together, and during rehearsals I noticed one of the cameramen becoming more and more disconcerted as he gazed through his lens at the Strad's aged front. Finally, he could bear it no longer.

'Cor, blimey!' he exclaimed in disgust. 'You'd think 'e'd 'ave bothered to buy a new one for the *TV*!'

The days when a soloist spent his professional life just touring concert halls have long since disappeared. Today, few weeks in the year go by without a visit to the studios — be it for making records or working on television or radio. In fact I have always considered recording to be a very important part of my work: records are left for posterity for future generations to judge from afar. It is a daunting prospect and a thought which has always made me try as hard as possible to make my recordings special. Sometimes I feel I have succeeded, sometimes not — only time will tell.

Much to my surprise my recording career began almost as soon as I left college, thanks to Peter Gammond — the editor of *Hi-Fi News* magazine. Peter had been asked by the educational label, Discourses, to mastermind a series of records featuring different instruments, and approached me to make the cello album.

It certainly resulted in a crash course on the pitfalls of recording! Because of its excellent acoustics we decided to make the LP at the church of St George the Martyr, Holborn. What we failed to realise was that, apart from the considerable traffic noise which spoilt many takes, an Italian restaurant had decided to open next door. With its kitchen backing on to the vestry — which had temporarily been converted into a control room — frequent forays had to be made to encourage their volatile chef to shout his orders a little more *sotto voce*. This wasn't easy and I have a feeling that if my knowledge of Italian had extended beyond a smattering of musical terms, the record would never have been completed!

Both of my next recordings were made at St John's, Smith Square, London — the church with sumptuous acoustics which the BBC has made a home for lunch-hour recitals. St John's is a great place to record, especially for solo cello, and both records — one, of modern British music with pianist-composer John McCabe, and the second, of John Ireland's piano trios — went more or less without a hitch — despite a sudden spasm of road drilling on one take.

My first recording with an orchestra was Frank Bridge's extraordinary *Concerto Elegiaco* or *Oration* as it is better known, although this masterly work is hardly known at all. Bridge was a highly original composer who, during the course of his life, underwent an almost total change of style. In his early days he made popular arrangements of songs like 'Sally in our Alley' and 'Cherry Ripe', but he gradually developed an advanced musical language clearly destined for unpopularity in the British musical climate of his time. *Oration* (1930) is a part of that musical language which perhaps explains, if not excuses, its failure to be recorded for forty-seven years. It is a fine work and I was more than determined to do it justice. But its obscurity meant that neither the orchestra — the London Philharmonic, nor the conductor — Nicholas Braithwaite, nor myself had ever played the piece before.

Now the cost of recording with a full orchestra is very expensive, so only one afternoon and evening were set aside to complete this difficult and unfamiliar score. I became increasingly worried about the whole thing: it would, after all, be my first orchestral recording.

As luck would have it Pierre Fournier — my teacher in Geneva — was giving a concert in London the night before and Celia felt this would be 'just the thing to take your mind off the recording'. But I couldn't face the thought of hearing a cello that night and — much to Celia's horror — took myself off to Millwall to see Orient's League Cup match! As Millwall is not renowned for being the most gentle of football grounds I think Celia feared my vociferous support for the O's might result in my returning home minus a couple of fingers. However, the diabolical refereeing decisions that evening — as the lads battled to yet another heroic goal-less bore — proved just the preparation I needed to set about the next day's recording with a vengeance!

Orient were also indirectly responsible for my next album, *Variations*. A greater contrast with *Oration* could scarcely be imagined, but it is just this sort of variety I have cherished during my career. I should think the sales figures were fairly different as well — *Variations* winning a gold disc within five weeks of release.

I had wanted my brother Andrew to write a piece using the cello for several years, both because of his gift for writing tunes and because I felt he would approach the cello in a new and creative way. For a while he stalled on the idea, basically because he wasn't sure the cello could be made to work with rock instruments and because he was busy with other projects.

In the end the decision whether or not to go ahead with the piece rested on a bet between us on the outcome of Orient's final match of the 1976–77 season against Hull City! There was a time when Andrew used to go to many Orient matches, but his patience had finally worn thin (a fundamental case of disloyalty). That season the O's were in a not unfamiliar position — they had to get at least a draw in their final home match to remain in the Second Division. Andrew was not convinced they could even manage that, but I *knew* the lads would pull through.

The bet was that if Orient managed to draw, or even win, then Andrew would finally have to write the piece. In true *Roy of the Rovers* style Orient battled to a nail-biting 1–1 draw and so *Variations* was finally born.

Apart from the many heart-stopping moments when

Orient nearly lost the match, *Variations* might never have happened for another reason — a blazing row between the two of us following its first performance. A superb collection of musicians had been assembled for the re-cording — drummer Jon Hiseman, his wife Barbara Thompson on flute and saxophone, Rod Argent and Don Airey on keyboards, and Gary Moore and John Mole on lead and bass guitars.

Before going into the studio we decided to try the piece live at the summer festival Andrew holds at his home every year. *Variations* was to be the second part of a morning cello recital — in the first half I would play sonatas with my pianist, Yitkin Seow. We rehearsed *Variations* like men possessed, and when the big day arrived both of us were thoroughly on edge.

Yitkin was playing in Belfast the night before and to arrive in time for our 11.30 performance depended on catching the first 'shuttle' flight. The whole point of the 'shuttle' is that if the first plane is full, another auto-matically follows to take the remaining passengers, but Yitkin arrived at the airport to find all seats on the first plane taken and no sign of any back-up flight. The only alternative to London was supplied — naturally enough — by British Midland Airways which, you will recall, is the only airline to guarantee my cello a seat. The trouble was that by the time their flight arrived there was no chance of Yitkin being there for the concert.

To fill in time we played *Variations* twice which, with hindsight, proved a godsend, as it gave the record people another chance to hear the piece and adjust to the then highly unusual combination of a cello with rock band.

Yitkin, meanwhile, was dashing to meet us, but by the time he arrived Andrew was so furious he refused to speak to him. This sent *me* into a rage and I heard myself saying I wanted nothing more to do with his project and would leave immediately. I tore upstairs to collect my things closely followed by Celia who — by some stroke of genius — managed to restore the peace.

Many people seem to think the success of *Variations* was a foregone conclusion, but certainly Andrew and I never saw it that way. To us, the idea of a cellist working on Paganini Variations with a rock band was a pretty long shot for commercial success, and a less enterprising record executive than MCA's Roy Featherstone might well have not encouraged the project so wholeheartedly.

By one of those strange coincidences my first inkling of the album's phenomenal success came the very day my life turned full circle and I played the Dvořák Concerto for an Ernest Read Children's Concert in the Royal Festival Hall. My first sight of a cello had been at one of these concerts and it was a moving moment when, as soon as the concerto was over, I was surrounded by hoards of inquisitive youngsters all demanding to know about the cello themselves. On the way back from the hall, I decided to drop into the Sloane Square branch of W.H. Smith to see whether they had *Variations* in stock yet. To my amazement there it was, proudly sitting at Number 8 on their LP chart — only the day after release! I rushed home to telephone Andrew with the news.

Quite apart from that nerve-racking incident with the chair at the Royal Variety Performance, *Variations* provided me with its fair share of 'firsts' — my first miming to a pre-recorded tape (on the *South Bank Show*), my first performance to a backing track (at the Society of West End Theatre Awards) and my first — and almost certainly last — performance in the Orient goalmouth!

Somehow Orient seem to have been involved all along the line with *Variations*, so when Andrew became the surprise victim of *This Is Your Life* the researchers came up with the bright idea of getting me to play a bit of it sitting in one of their goals. Then for a laugh a player would shoot the ball past me into the net! This is where the problems started. Unfortunately, the dummy cello specially constructed for this spectacular got stuck in the traffic and, as the daylight faded, it looked as though the whole idea would have to be abandoned — unless I would agree to use my

90

own precious instrument. The TV crew seemed none too concerned about my predicament but, unlike me, they didn't know the lads' shooting abilities! After much agonising I agreed and, with the cello decked out in Orient scarves and rosettes, the cameras rolled. Shaking both with cold and fear, I waited for the dreadful moment when the ball would come hurtling towards us. But my worries were unfounded – as the ball not only missed the cello but the goal altogether.

However, the hardest of all those 'firsts' was playing to that backing track at the Society of West End Theatre Awards. Not only were the whole proceedings being televised live, but the dinner was packed with show business luminaries from Roy Hudd to Richard Harris, and it is never easy to play to an audience of fellow 'pros'. Most of all, I had been brought up on that all-important eye contact with other musicians and found just playing to a tape strangely unspontaneous.

Variations was also responsible for one more unforgettable moment. As Orient had, in a sense, been the cause of the whole project, MCA made a special gold disc for the club which I presented to their chairman on the pitch before the match with Leicester City. It was undoubtedly the proudest moment of my life.

Not long before the release of *Variations*, I signed up to make a record called *The Romantic Cello* with a new classical company — Enigma Records, run by John Boyden, who had had great success with the Classics for Pleasure label. It was to be a collection of short, romantic pieces and — as on my very first recording — a church was chosen in preference to a studio for its warmer sound.

If the sound was warmer, the temperature was not! Yitkin and I arrived on a freezing February morning smothered in jerseys and overcoats, and took the added precaution of bringing a small two-bar electric fire. It was all to no avail. The church was like an ice-box and fearful spittings and cracklings soon put a stop to our attempts at using both bars of the fire at once.

Between takes we desperately hurried to and from the remainder of the fire to try and coax some life back into our stiffened fingers. Even then birds chirruped away on several of our better takes and we began to long for the warmth and quiet of a studio. In the end *The Romantic Cello* proved to be a popular album, but I have to say that of all my recordings it is my least favourite.

Soon after making a second record with Yitkin for Enigma — of Debussy and Rachmaninov — the label was acquired by the giant consortium WEA, whose commitment to the classics might best have been judged by their hit single of the moment — the *Winkers Song* (*Misprint*) by Ivor Biggun. Predictably, it wasn't long before Enigma was shut down; not, however, before I had managed to make one more record for them — one that still remains very special to me. This was the première recording of Benjamin Britten's superb *Third Suite for Cello* (a piece written for Rostropovich), together with music by two of Britten's teachers — Frank Bridge's *Elegy* and John Ireland's hauntingly beautiful *Sonata*.

Happily, the Enigma catalogue was soon made available once more by another enterprising British label — ASV Records — but that experience does go to show what little control an artist has over an album once it has been made. So, despite my belief in the lasting importance of recordings, there are certainly problems involved — particularly with classical music.

Some of the larger record companies are increasingly dominated by accountants who, in many cases, have no idea how a classical record works or can be made to work. They tend to judge the success of any new release on the sales figures it achieves in its first few weeks but, unlike many pop albums — which are here today and gone tomorrow — a good classical LP can continue to sell over a very long period of time — sometimes for up to twenty-five years. In this quick turnover world of disposable goods, some classical records are removed from the catalogue almost before their reviews have had time to appear in the monthly magazines.

Recording is certainly a technique on its own. I prefer to work with as few takes as possible so that editing is reduced to a minimum. Then the flavour of a live performance, with all its spontaneity, remains.

This was particularly brought home to me when recording Delius's *Caprice and Elegy* with Eric Fenby and the Royal Philharmonic Orchestra. Since this was one of the works Delius had actually dictated to Fenby, the recording was already a remarkable experience — but the *Caprice and*

Elegy was only part of a two-record set of Delius's music and the recording time was rapidly running out. There was no alternative — it had to be done in one take and it had to be good. Yet the pressure of the occasion worked to good advantage and it remains one of my favourite recordings.

Early in my career I discovered how easily the slightest extraneous sound is picked up by sensitive microphones. Even so, by the time I came to record my first album for RCA — *Cello Man* — I had still not learned to stop my right foot thudding on the studio floor. Eventually their very experienced producer, Charles Gerhardt, persuaded me to record most of the album barefoot (although I can still detect the occasional thud on Bruch's *Kol Nidrei*!).

Other musicians might not have been so obliging. Sir Adrian Boult once told me what happened when he recorded the Elgar Concerto with Pablo Casals. Unfortunately Casals' legendary grunting was coming through loud and clear, to the point where the distraught recording engineer could contain himself no longer.

'Maestro,' he protested, 'I'm afraid we're picking up all your grunts.'

'In that case,' replied Casals, singularly unmoved, 'you can charge double for the record!'

Many musicians feel one of their most nerve-racking experiences is broadcasting a concert live on radio, especially as many people tape these performances — illegally or otherwise — for closer analysis afterwards. Not only are you totally dependent on the whims of a radio engineer for the sort of balance and sound that comes over but, of course, the listener at home remains blissfully unaware of the atmosphere in the concert hall.

I vividly remember playing a lunchtime recital for BBC Radio 3 from Bradford Library Theatre. Free admission was allowed to these concerts — a policy which was no doubt very socially aware, but which also resulted in some highly strange characters wandering in to escape from the

94

*The traditional handshake with Her Majesty The Queen following the Royal Variety
Performance* (Photo: PPS)

*Rehearsing the Elgar Concerto with Sir Georg Solti and the London
Philharmonic Orchestra* (Photo: Tom Ang)

Left, *With Stephane Grappelli outside the Royal Festival Hall* (Photo: The Times)

Opposite, top, *With Eric Fenby after a run-through of the Delius Sonata* (Photo: David Ingham)

Opposite, below, *On TV with Cleo Laine* (Photo: Yorkshire Television)

Right, *On the lakeside at San Ramon with Joaquin Rodrigo* (Photo: Clive Barda)

A moving moment as the Rodrigos (bottom right) hear Joaquin's Concerto *for the first time* (Photo: Clive Barda)

Discussing Vaughan Williams's Fantasia on Sussex Folk Tunes *at a recording session with Vernon Handley and the composer's widow Ursula* (Photo: Erica Creer)

rain, wind or whatever other acts of God happened to be around Bradford during the lunch hour. No sooner had I begun the ethereal slow movement of Beethoven's D major Sonata — one of the deepest (and quietest) in music — than a somewhat bedraggled lady tramp shambled into the theatre, muttering all the while, and set off down the gangway towards me. Plonking herself noisily in the front row, she pulled from her pocket a packet of crisps. Each time the music paused — pregnant with meaning — I was deafened by the crunch of her salt 'n vinegars. Surely I would have to stop — her antics must be ruining my performance. But I had a nagging suspicion that this nasty incident would be going by unnoticed over the air and that an outburst about crisps would seem strangely inappropriate. I soldiered on.

Sure enough, when I got home and listened to the tape, the cacophony hadn't registered.

Radio interviews are, on the whole, not nearly such a cause for alarm. Undoubtedly the worst I have ever known was one I did with Andrew on a local station just after *Variations* was released. It went something like this:

'Julian. You've just been appointed a Professor of Cello at the Guildhall School of Music. Why didn't you write the music for the album yourself?'

'I wanted Andrew to write it.'

'I see. Now Andrew, how come you haven't used Tim Rice on this piece?'

'Because there aren't any words.' And so on.

However British broadcasters are usually among the best in the world and many who have interviewed me, such as Richard Baker, Jimmy Savile or Gloria Hunniford, are superbly professional. Nevertheless, things can still go wrong. On Pete Murray's *Open House*, I proudly introduced Falla's *Ritual Fire Dance* from the *Cello Man* LP as a 'wild, demonic piece' — only for the record to be cued in at half speed!

I was even more embarrassed on WQXR in New York. After discussing Popper's 'fiendish' *Elfin Dance*, the announcer took up my words in a racy crescendo:

'And now we'll hear what Julian Lloyd Webber describes

95

as one of the fastest, most technically difficult pieces of music ever written for the cello.' Over the airwaves drifted the dulcet tones of *The Swan*. To make matters worse the presenter was too embarrassed to take it off, although he did manage to mumble an apology at the end.

My introduction to television was not without mishap either. Towards the end of my student days, Dutch television had contacted all the British music colleges and auditioned hundreds of aspiring young soloists, myself included, for their new series, *Brilliant Young Musicians from Around the World*. Apparently it would be a marvellous opportunity as the programmes had built up a massive audience.

When the letter arrived with the news that I, along with two singers, had been chosen to represent Britain, I immediately started agonising over what I should play on such a vital occasion — it would obviously have to be something pretty impressive. The TV people decided for me. They particularly wanted Haydn's Concerto in D, one of the hardest pieces in a cellist's repertoire — with a finale which has become a legendary graveyard for nervous performers.

Having understandably failed in my repeated attempts to get Haydn changed to Shostakovich, I set about my practice fiendishly, and began to long for the moment when it would all be over and I could relax once again. After several days' rehearsal in Holland preparations were complete and, as I took the platform, I felt a strange sense of ease — tonight nothing was going to go wrong. My confidence grew and grew and by the time the finale arrived I was thoroughly enjoying myself negotiating its notorious pitfalls with abandon. A storm of applause greeted the last chords and, after taking my bows, I was embraced by a beaming producer who pronounced the performance 'perfect'.

Elated, I packed up my cello and set off to the bar for a long glass of beer. Several long glasses later the producer — still beaming — arrived beside me, seemingly to join in my celebrations.

'The performance was magnificent,' he declared. 'We've watched the whole thing through and you were just wonderful.' My senses reeled both with pleasure and increasingly severe inebriation. He continued: 'But we had a little trouble with the pictures towards the end and I'm afraid there's no alternative but to take the finale again. Please be back on the studio floor in five minutes.'

I do not recall the retake but I'm told that through some extraordinary combination of good fortune and alcohol everything, including the pictures, slotted into place.

Since that inauspicious beginning I have worked on a wide range of television, from variety shows with established stars such as Sasha Distel and Cleo Laine, chat shows with Michael Parkinson and Russell Harty to Arts programmes like the *South Bank Show* and *Omnibus*. On one occasion I appeared on the *Marti Caine Show*. Marti is certainly an attractive lady and — as she is inclined to do — wore a fairly revealing evening dress on the programme. Shortly after-wards I received a hysterical letter from one of the congregation at the Methodist Central Hall, Westminster where, for many years, my father was organist. The writer declared that I was 'a disgrace to my father's name' and should never have appeared on such a disgusting, satanic piece of 'popular' entertainment. He was sure that Dr Lloyd Webber would agree. What was unknown to the writer was that I had watched the programme with my father and closely observed his reactions first hand. He was chuckling throughout.

It appears that any classical musician who tries to bring his art to a wider audience is open to criticism, but it is so much easier to stay in an ivory tower and preach to the converted. I think it is my duty to enable people from all walks of life and society to hear the instrument which means so much to me and, if I feel like encouragement, I only need to look as far as the great composer Shostakovich, who summed up my feelings perfectly: 'I consider that every artist who isolates himself from the world is doomed. I find it incredible that an artist should wish to shut himself

97

away from the people. I always try to make myself as widely understood as possible and if I don't succeed I consider it my own fault.'

Occasionally television producers are inclined to put pictures before music and this can lead to flashy experiments which have to be curbed before it's too late. Once I arrived armed with the cellist's *pièce de resistance*, Popper's *Elfin Dance*. This piece has the disturbing habit of continually whizzing up the fingerboard to such stratospheres of pitch that only a bat can fully appreciate the achievement. For this cellists' Everest the producer dreamed up an ace idea — a small beam of light would pursue my left hand up and down the cello. No further lighting would be needed. But sadly the lighting man could not keep up with me, frequently focusing on empty stretches of fingerboard while my left hand probed the darkness beyond. It was a fiasco and 'normal' lighting had to be restored immediately.

Sometimes — in the interests of good television — extraordinary combinations of guests are gathered. One of the oddest line-ups I've ever known was when Eric Fenby and myself appeared on a programme about Delius with Kate Bush and Russell Harty. Kate had included a song about Delius on one of her LPs, and Russell thought it would be 'fun' to spring her typically zany video of the number on Eric to get his reaction. Fortunately, Dr Fenby was at his most diplomatic:

'I think Delius would have found it a most gracious tribute,' he said with a knowing smile.

Television has enabled me to work with some great artists outside the world of music. I have fond memories of smashing Kenny Everett over the head with a dummy cello when he gave a truly excruciating rendition of *The Swan* on his show but, unluckily, I was unable to perpetrate a further act of aggression planned for Tim Rice.

Tim was another guest on Harry Secombe's show and, as well as playing, I was asked to join in a sketch where Rice was to take the part, appropriately enough, of a bad pub pianist. This eventually ended with everyone pouring a pint of beer over his head. Now this had been a fond ambition of mine ever since, back in Harrington Court days, he had mutilated the cover of one of my Bobby Vee LPs. To be able to realise this in front of millions (and, what's more, be paid for the privilege) seemed too good to be true. But on reaching Yorkshire Television it appeared that the technicians had gone on strike due to 'fleas in the studio' and it was a case of 'everybody out' until the entire set had been fumigated. By the time this was done an item had to be cut, so Tim remained — unlike the fleas — one jump ahead.

One ambition I was able to realise was to work with Olympic gold medallist Robin Cousins. Robin had heard me play *The Swan* and wanted to skate to my performance of it. A further piece called *Swan Variations* was specially composed for the programme and Robin was shown at work choreographing the music, with brilliant results. The ballerina Pavlova became famous for her interpretation of *The Swan*, but I believe Robin's would have compared well with her great performance.

Whatever the programme I always like to play if possible, as the cello is so much a part of me that I sometimes feel strangely lost without it. Standing in the wings, I remember being gripped with a sudden sense of panic as my name was announced as guest on *Face the Music*. Where was my cello? I had left it behind! . . . But, of course, this was one time in my life it was not needed.

Another non-playing incident, which certainly didn't achieve the desired effect, occurred during the *South Bank Show*'s documentary on the creation and first performance of the Concerto that Joaquin Rodrigo wrote for me. I had been looking forward to receiving the Concerto for ages and Alan Benson, the programme's director, was determined to be in right at the start to film my instant reactions on seeing the music. I swore that I would phone him as soon as it arrived, and Celia was also made to promise she would prevent me from opening the long-awaited envelope. The morning it eventually came I was setting off on tour, so — not being allowed to take it with me — I spent a troubled few days wondering what was in store for me.

Finally, the TV entourage arrived in my living-room to capture this historic moment for all time. With the cameras rolling, I tore open the envelope and gazed incredulously at the score, while exclaiming at the difficulty of some of Rodrigo's passagework. Ironically when the programme was shown, everyone thought my bewildered reactions had been faked!

Television has certainly given me some odd moments, but perhaps my most bizarre experience with the media came from a film company who were, they said, keen to interest me in accepting my first movie rôle. Both the producer and director had already been to see me at the Festival Hall and were now firmly convinced that only *I* could play the part. Intrigued, I sent for the script.

It was a lurid little ditty about a cellist who, during the course of the film, somehow managed to infect the entire cast – both male and female – with syphilis.

I still can't think why they thought of me.

The explosions of temperament for which musicians are renowned are often just another way of relieving tension — as the lighting man at Snape Maltings was to discover when Sir Clifford Curzon arrived to give a series of concerts at the Benson and Hedges Chamber Music Festival. From the first the lighting was evidently not to Sir Clifford's taste. Apparently there was a terrible glare coming back off his music; then a spotlight was shining straight in his eyes; then light was reflecting from the keyboard. With admirable patience the hapless electrician worked his way through every conceivable permutation of lighting — each one provoking a further burst of wrath from Sir Clifford. Eventually, after more than an hour spent in vain, the distraught engineer admitted defeat and set the lights back to their original position.

'That's it!' cried Sir Clifford. 'That's how I want it. Why couldn't you have set them like that in the first place?'

That superb violinist Itzhak Perlman belongs at the other end of the temperamental scale. We shared a dressing-room during the Royal Variety Performance and I was astonished at how relaxed he appeared just before going on stage. By some extraordinary quirk of back-stage chatter the conversation turned to Bobby Vee, and Itzhak's uncalled-for, if spirited, burst into voice with *Take Good Care*

Of My Baby has, disturbingly, proved unforgettable. At the performance he appeared sublimely at ease. It was only later that he revealed he had a splitting headache, which became so bad that he was forced to miss the traditional handshake with the Queen. Perhaps he, too, was suffering from the tension of the occasion, but if so he concealed it as brilliantly as he played.

Nowadays the sort of schedules required of top musicians can all too easily result in complete exhaustion, so it is vital for the soloist to have as wide a range of interests outside the profession as possible.

Turtles are fairly far removed from cello-playing, and we used to have two — Boosey and Hawkes. Sadly, only Boosey is still with us. We call him Boosey as, whenever he's allowed out of his tank, he heads straight towards my large collection of beer bottles which lie in wait on the kitchen floor. These bring me to another interest. In order to understand fully the minds of composers such as Elgar, Holst and John Ireland, it is obviously essential to try out the various tipples they might well have enjoyed — hence my interest in regional ales. And it has to be said that the thought of imbibing such excellent brews as Thwaites, Robinsons or Mitchells and Butlers post-performance has added extra spice to many a concert in far-flung corners of the British Isles.

Distressingly, news of my hobby has leaked out. After a concert in Yorkshire with Simon Nicholls we were invited to the home of some highly orthodox Methodists who were obviously determined to restrict our liquid intake to a cup of tea. As closing time approached desperate measures were called for; after a brief discussion, we agreed our tactics. Simon had left his music on top of the piano — we would just nip back to the hall and get it: 'It will only take a few minutes'.

An hour later we returned, suitably refreshed but, in our absence, Celia had phoned. I rang her straight back.

'Did you have a nice drink?' she asked. 'They told me you'd gone to the pub.'

Concerts can certainly be a terrible distraction from the truly important things in life — like football. For one thing they consistently take place on a Saturday, which makes it quite impossible to go to that mecca of football, Brisbane Road. Many a vital fixture has been rudely interrupted by rehearsals and things, and if it were not for the BBC's comprehensive soccer coverage on the World Service, many foreign tours would obviously have had to be cancelled altogether.

Sometimes the news of a famous victory can prove a wonderful inspiration for the evening's performance. Only recently I was glued to the radio in my Lisbon hotel, waiting with baited breath to hear whether or not Orient had finally been relegated to the Fourth Division. I can hardly think what effect such a catastrophe might have had on my playing, but in the event the lads' magnificent 4–1 win inspired my performance to renewed heights at the International Gulbenkian Festival. This link between football and music is not as unusual as it may seem. Most symphony orchestras have their own football teams and even the conductors sometimes join in — the LSO maestro Claudio Abbado, for example, is a notorious football fanatic.

It is also a good idea for a soloist to develop a few solitary hobbies to help while away some of the lonelier moments on tour, and computer chess, reading and even CB radio have become popular pastimes. These certainly prove less of a distraction than that little-known phenomenon, the classical groupie — or 'green room vultures' as they are termed in the profession. Many of these have a vague connection with the music business which they will ruthlessly exploit to catch their prey. Constantly they will claim to be 'terrific friends' with all the world's most famous musicians but, more often than not, friendship will have played no part in their relationships. Nonetheless, it has to be said that musicians have not, on the whole, proved unwilling victims of these predators. Whoever said 'Music might tame and civilise wild beasts, but 'tis evident it has never yet tamed and civilised musicians' obviously had inside knowledge of the music business as, from Paganini to Rubinstein, musical

103

history is littered with the amorous exploits of its composers and performers. Yet these affairs tend to be brief, unhappy liaisons. To remain at the top of his profession a soloist needs to be constantly alert and at one with himself and if anything, or anyone, disrupts this fine tuning for any length of time, there will be trouble.

Intense pressure can often be made to work to advantage, even if its source is far removed from music. After playing Strauss's *Don Quixote* on tour with the Royal Liverpool Philharmonic Orchestra, they asked me to repeat it at their Royal Festival Hall concert three months later. As this would be only my second performance at the Festival Hall I knew only too well how nervous I would be. So I decided to give myself something else to worry about and get married the next day.

I asked Celia what she thought of the idea and, astonished by her reply, started breaking the news. My agents were horrified — they thought my full attention should be directed towards the concert. But I was confident that I knew the Strauss well and was sure that the added distraction would be a good thing.

As it happened the plan nearly backfired. In many ways my preparation for the concert had been ideal. Not only was I working with the conductor, Sir Charles Groves, on the Strauss, but we also had a performance of the Elgar together in Nottingham just a few days earlier. But the musician's nightmare nearly came true — I almost forgot the music. All my life I have been very lucky with musical memory, finding that by the time I know the notes of a piece I have also memorised it. However I have also learned that the more you worry about remembering a piece the more likely you are to forget it — and this was precisely my mistake on this occasion.

Suddenly, in the middle of some passagework, I started to wonder which note came next and, for a terrible moment, my mind went blank. Instinctively, I let my fingers take over, praying they would automatically go to the notes I had been practising so hard for the past few weeks. After what seemed an eternity, but was probably only a few bars, my nerve steadied — and I was back in control.

It is hard to convey just how lonely and desolate it feels on the platform when something does go wrong. Unlike an actor, the soloist has no prompt. The spotlight is on *you* and if everything goes wrong it is *your fault* — there is no one else to blame. Every soloist, no matter how great, has had to survive such ordeals. One well-known violinist came to grief in a duo recital with Rachmaninov at Carnegie Hall. Very often the string player will play from memory, whereas his pianist uses the music and on this occasion the violinist lost his way during a Beethoven Sonata. Sidling over to the piano, he attempted to catch a glimpse of the music.

'Where are we?' he whispered frantically to Rachmaninov.

'Carnegie Hall,' said the pianist.

A happy side-effect of great pressure is that the concerts on either side of the 'big occasion' seem relatively relaxed and the Dvořák — that most supreme of concertos — has often figured in my diary either just before or just after great landmarks in my career. I have fond memories of playing it with James Conlon and the LPO immediately after the première of the Rodrigo Concerto; with Norman Del Mar and the Philharmonia a few days before my New York début; and with Svetlanov and the LSO at the Barbican only a week before my first concerts with the Berlin Philharmonic. Although these 'Dvořáks' were important concerts, they did not have such career significance, so I was able to relax and revel in the wonders of Dvořák's masterpiece.

Sometimes a run of important concerts helps take the mind off one specific date. For example, after returning from a lengthy tour one Sunday night I took part in the Royal Variety Performance on the Monday, a televised Schools Prom on the Tuesday and played a Haydn Concerto at the Queen Elizabeth Hall on the Wednesday. At times like these a curious sense of peace comes over me, almost as if I have slipped into a different gear. When the pace slackens the exertion takes its toll but, when I need it most, I have my protective shield.

Nervous tension by no means has the same effect on all performers. One night when I was feeling particularly nervous before a live broadcast of the Elgar, I happened to ask Raymond Leppard, the conductor, if he had ever known a soloist chicken out at the last minute. Apparently it had happened to that very orchestra only a few months before, when a lady violinist was supposed to be giving a live broadcast of the Beethoven Concerto. Moments before the start she was nowhere to be found and a search party was launched. Eventually she was tracked down to the Ladies, from which sanctuary she adamantly refused to budge. Cunning tactics were obviously required, so the producer paraded up and down the corridor, loudly announcing that the concerto was cancelled and the orchestra should now proceed straight to the New World Symphony. The trick paid off and the ashen-faced violinist emerged for the performance, still steadfastly refusing to play the cadenza — which she replaced with a little trill that somehow brought the orchestra back in.

It is not always easy to make the right decisions under extreme pressure and there have certainly been times when, with more time to think clearly, I might have acted differently. Once, in the middle of a rehearsal of the Elgar Concerto in Manchester, I was hauled to the telephone to give a snap decision on whether I would stand in for a Festival Hall performance of Shostakovich's First Concerto. I had never played the Shostakovich in public before and it turned out there would be only one day to practise it. In a moment of madness I agreed. What my agents failed to mention was that the performance was also being broadcast live!

With a little more time for reflection I am sure that I would have talked myself into believing that the Shostakovich could not be prepared in one day, but — having accepted the date — I had to go through with it.

It was a blessing I did, as that performance led directly to the offer of a recording contract with RCA.

Artists respond to great tension in many different ways, often needing a safety valve that enables them to let off steam. A few days before a performance of the Elgar with Sir Georg Solti at the Royal Festival Hall (which was the first time he had ever conducted it), I went to his home to prepare for the concert. It was fascinating to work so closely with Sir Georg on a concerto I had played many times but which was completely fresh to him. I was able to observe at close quarters the way he approached a masterpiece, free from any preconceived ideas, and I enjoyed our collaboration enormously.

Yet, in spite of our detailed rehearsal, I was amused by the attention he lavished on his central heating system, which seemed to have broken down alarmingly. As various heating engineers struggled with the repairs, Sir Georg barked directions at them which were every bit as forceful as those given to his orchestra.

My reaction to the pressure of the Festival Hall concert was slightly different, as once again, I agreed to give an important performance the night before (a televised Schools Prom at the Albert Hall). For me this would be the perfect build-up to one of the most exciting dates in my career.

I have always enjoyed working with artists from different areas of the music world. Certainly the top jazz and rock musicians are every bit as talented as their classical counterparts and I have learned as much about the arts of phrasing and performance from great artists such as Cleo Laine and Stephane Grappelli as anyone. Their natural approach to music is free and unstifled. Stephane, for example, has never had a violin lesson in his life, yet he is a true virtuoso. Gary Moore — the lead guitarist on *Variations* — is likewise completely self-taught but, apart from his stunning technique, he possesses a musical memory which would be the envy of many a classical musician. Composer-performers like Peter Skellern and John Dankworth had lengthy formal trainings at music college, but they both took a conscious decision to make their careers outside the classical field. Both Peter and John have composed for me and I hope to continue to explore all avenues in my quest for new cello music.

Music must never be allowed to stagnate, so that the only music we hear in the concert hall is by dead composers. But the trouble with a lot of today's so-called 'classical' cello music is that it is singularly ill-suited to the instrument. The cello has a massive pitch-span of more than five and a half octaves, and many exciting possibilities for the instrument are just waiting to be explored. As a lyrical instrument the cello is unsurpassed, and unlike some 'avant-garde' composers (who seem happier to see you bang it on the side, bow the wrong side of the bridge, swivel it round or do anything, in fact, except actually play it) rock composers could use the cello to great advantage.

One festival I played at had the bright idea of running a competition to find a new piece for solo cello. All the entries would be sent to me and I would choose the winner — who would receive a performance of his composition and a cheque to go with it.

After wading through reams and reams of 'music' which, with its trendy signs and symbols, might have found better use as wallpaper, I finally stumbled across a piece I really did like. The trouble was that in one passage the cellist was instructed to dash all over the fingerboard at breakneck speed while apparently plucking his open C string at the same time. Having failed miserably with my solemn attempts to perform this feat, Hendrix-style, with my teeth, only two alternatives remained. Either a second cellist would have to be brought in at great expense, or someone would have to wait patiently behind me to pluck when required. We settled on the latter solution and Celia was brought in to make her concert début (only later did we remember that she does not belong to the Musicians' Union!). If the cello writing in this piece was not entirely practical, Celia's sudden appearance on stage certainly helped to remove the stuffy atmosphere which often prevails at concerts of modern music.

During a concert of 'contemporary works' at St John's, Smith Square, the atmosphere reached such heights of oppression that even my cello had a seizure and promptly broke one of its strings. I changed the string as quickly as possible and returned to the platform, hoping the accident might have helped relieve the gloom. But it felt more like a morgue than ever and, in a desperate, misguided attempt to inject some humour into the situation I cheerfully remarked:

'It's always useful to have a spare G string with you.'

109

There was an awful silence, and I quickly sat down to resume my piece, feeling thoroughly disgraced.

The formal atmosphere at some classical concerts — especially those ones where the audience are better dressed than the performers — undoubtedly keeps many people away from the concert hall. After a recital at the Newcastle Festival I repaired to a down-at-heel pub near the hall with my cello — the sight of which immediately prompted the usual flow of remarks of the 'look out — he's on the fiddle' variety (and not a few others besides). When the hubbub eventually died down I was surrounded by inquisitive Geordies — who are nothing if not direct.

'I thought about going to the concert tonight,' said one, 'but I wouldn't have enjoyed all that upper-class music.'

Despite my attempts to persuade him otherwise, nothing could shake his belief that you had to 'dress up' for classical concerts and know all about music in order to appreciate it. He could not have been more wrong. Great music is not the preserve of a privileged or wealthy élite. It is an international language that cuts across barriers of race and class. 'I love music passionately,' said Debussy, 'and because I love it I try to free it from the barren traditions which stifle it. Music should be a free art, gushing forth, an open air art, an art boundless as the elements, the wind, the sky and the sea.' What happy words!

I feel the same about interpretation. Far rather, for me, the heartwarming commitment of a Rostropovich than the academic detachment of some lesser players. Rostropovich has occasionally been accused of excess — of perhaps giving the music almost more than it can take, but I feel he has always put the wishes of the composer first — unlike some performers, who seem more concerned with projecting themselves than the music.

Music should come from the heart, be played from the heart and go straight to the heart. Dry, sterile music designed for a fashionable minority holds no interest for me.

110

The most sensitive musical partnership of all is probably the one between conductor and soloist. While many conductors enjoy working with a soloist and the close music-making this brings, there are undoubtedly a few who regard soloists as an unwelcome intrusion — people who waste valuable rehearsal time which, they think, would be much better spent on their overtures and symphonies. Mercifully, these 'maestri' form a tiny minority for a conductor who feels this way can easily wreck a concerto performance. Back in the days of Haydn and Mozart a conductor wasn't considered necessary for concertos, and the soloist would direct the performance himself. This still works well on these early pieces and I especially enjoyed taking that rôle during my recording of Haydn concertos with the English Chamber Orchestra, when the players sat around my rostrum in a semi-circle, establishing an immediate rapport.

From my many enjoyable partnerships with conductors I think I would especially single out working on the Elgar with Sir Georg Solti and recording the effervescent Lalo Concerto with Jesús López-Cobos, and of the British conductors both Sir John Pritchard and Vernon Handley are exceptionally sympathetic. I am very sad to have missed playing with Sir Adrian Boult. We were going to broadcast the Saint-Saëns Concerto together as part of a programme to celebrate the fiftieth birthday of the BBC Symphony Orchestra. By this time Sir Adrian had already retired from conducting in the concert hall, but we all had high hopes that he would feel strong enough to undertake the studio recording. To our great disappointment it was not to be, but I was lucky enough to work closely with Sir Adrian on the Elgar — which he had studied with the composer many years before.

Russian conductors are always exciting to work with. Their technique is invariably superb and I find their balletic approach to conducting immensely invigorating. Yevgeny Svetlanov is a particularly excellent accompanist and I also enjoyed playing the Shostakovich No. 1 with Yuri Temirkanov. Very often the Soviet command of English is significantly better than they would have you believe. After my rehearsal with Yuri at the Henry Wood Hall, I took him for a drink. Just as he was attempting to explain how he spoke no English at all, the barman asked what he wanted to drink.

'A pint of Young's Special, please,' came the knowledgeable reply.

An instrumentalist's relationship with his pianist is of vital importance. Not only is a close musical understanding essential, but the partnership also has to work on a personal level. On tour you travel together, stay at the same hotels together and generally tread on each other's toes to an alarming degree.

Travelling with a cello certainly causes a few headaches but a pianist faces a set of problems all his own. What could be worse than arriving at a hall a few hours before the concert and finding the piano in terrible condition? Even a piano that has been overhauled can prove an unexpected hazard as I discovered — too late for comfort — at a rehearsal one afternoon in Blackheath. Working our way happily through a Beethoven Sonata, the proceedings were suddenly brought to a halt by an ear-splitting crash, followed by the sound of breaking piano strings and a whimpering pianist. Fleeing from the stage to the comparative safety of the concert hall, I gazed at the scene of destruction before me.

The piano lid had fallen in, narrowly missing the neck of my cello and, come to think of it, my own neck as well. Later the organisers told us that the piano had just returned from an overhaul at one of London's most famous stores, but obviously this had not extended to putting the pins back in the lid afterwards.

In a great deal of cello and piano music, the piano plays an equally important rôle and the word accompanist can prove dangerously emotive in the presence of one's pianist. One of the chief causes of argument between duo partners is likely to concern the question of balance between the two instruments. This especially applies to cello and piano music where the cello can find it hard to compete with the size and volume of a modern concert grand, particularly if the piano part is over-elaborate in the first place (and a lot of composers were pianists!).

I have been fortunate to have found such fine and sympathetic partners as Sir Clifford Curzon, Murray Perahia, John Lill, John McCabe, Yitkin Seow, Simon Nicholls and Eric Fenby, and I have certainly never reached the point of frustration evidently experienced by one famous cellist of his day when he played through a Brahms sonata with the composer himself at the piano.

Astonished by the torrents of sound exploding from the keyboard, the unfortunate cellist brought the proceedings to a halt.

'Dr Brahms!' he pleaded, 'I really can't hear myself play!'

'And,' growled the great composer, 'you don't know how lucky you are.'

The relationship between composer and performer is an endless source of fascination — a vital merging of creative personalities, where either one would be lost without the other. If the chemistry is right it can be the most artistically rewarding of all music partnerships and being a part of the creation of new works has given me some of the most exciting moments of my life.

From my first encounter with Sir Arthur Bliss I discovered that composers are not necessarily the wild, demonic figures portrayed in Hollywood movies*. More often than not the opposite is the case, and the very people you would have expected to be most critical about the way their music is played often seem content just to sit back and enjoy it.

Shortly after my unnerving experience with Sir Arthur, when he sat through my performance in virtual silence, I had a similar reaction from Peter Racine Fricker when he came to the rehearsals of his *Cello Sonata* which I was due to play on the South Bank. The Sonata is a complex, demanding work but he had little to say about my interpretation and again, while working with Sir Lennox Berkeley on the recording of his *Duo*, I found this same

---

* For example the wonderful Claude Rains–Bette Davis film *Deception*, is all about a new cello concerto by a manically egocentric composer.

reluctance to criticise. The truth is that — unless it differs wildly from theirs — most composers prefer a performer to develop an interpretation of his own.

Modesty is another, possibly unexpected, characteristic I have encountered in composers. When I was working on Andre Previn's *Cello Concerto* for a broadcast, I was surprised at his inclination to run the piece down, even though he did have more to say than most about interpretation. Likewise John McCabe, who gave me detailed (and extremely helpful) assistance at the recording of his cello *Partita*.

Geoffrey Burgon (who wrote such brilliantly effective music for the television serials *Brideshead Revisited* and *Tinker, Tailor, Soldier, Spy*) also dedicated a solo cello piece to me. I had first heard his music at the première of his *Requiem* and, much impressed, asked him if he would like to write me something for the cello. I soon discovered another aspect of composers' modesty. One evening Geoffrey rang me with the news that he had finished the piece and I arrived at his house with great expectations. The manuscript was sitting on top of the piano and Geoffrey explained he was going to attempt to give me a rough idea of how it went, but I would have to make allowances for his total lack of ability on the piano — whereupon he played the whole thing through note-perfectly!

However I must not leave composers with too untarnished an image because there are some resounding exceptions to this meek and mild approach to criticism — my brother Andrew being a prime example. What makes Andrew's criticisms doubly annoying is that they are nearly always right! I was on a long foreign tour when Andrew began work on *Variations*, so our conversations about its progress were restricted to one or two lengthy telephone calls. The idea of the piece being a set of variations on the well-known Paganini theme was entirely Andrew's and as so many composers, from Brahms to Rachmaninov, had already turned their attention to this famous theme, I thought he was taking quite a risk. But Andrew, who thrives on such challenges, pressed ahead regardless and I found the cello part awaiting my return.

That night I sat down and sight-read it through for the first time. I had no idea what to expect, but whatever hopes I did have were immediately surpassed. I remember my delight at the way Andrew ended Variation V, and my sense of wonder that he was constantly able to deliver such winning phrases. After years spent listening to my practice, Andrew had obviously thoroughly absorbed the capabilities of the cello because, apart from my adding some double-stopping in the final variation, only a few changes needed to be made.

I finished that first playthrough in a state of high excitement, but it was only later that I felt able to tell him I thought he had written the best music for cello since Britten. That night I don't think he would have believed me.

Andrew's sense of theatre was also much in evidence with his idea of winding the C string down to an A on the cello's final note. On stage it looks great!

There could not have been more contrast between our lengthy and detailed rehearsals on *Variations* and my collaboration with John Dankworth. After playing at Lord Rosehill's open air theatre at Fair Oak, in Sussex, the organisers asked if I would like to come back the following summer and première a new piece by the composer of my choice. It was too good an offer to refuse. As a long-time admirer of both John Dankworth and his wife, Cleo Laine, I suggested that they commission John (on the one condition that he would agree to play in the piece as well). The result was *Fair Oak Fusions*, named after Lord Rosehill's estate.

The only trouble was that two weeks before the first concert not a note of the piece had appeared. Embarrassingly we had agreed to do a radio interview around that time and, sure enough, the inevitable question was asked — how was the piece going? I listened to John's reply intently.

'Well, you know,' he said, 'I like working under pressure, and it's sort of coming along nicely in my mind.' With a week to go it remained in John's mind and bits and pieces were continuing to filter through on the day. Tragically, no sooner had the ink dried on the manuscript than it disappeared again! To protect us from the elements, these open-air concerts were held in what was called 'a specially-constructed superstructure' — in other words a tent. Sure enough, in the middle of the piece, a violent thunderstorm erupted which proved too much for even the expensive super-structure to bear and a severe leak developed roughly above my music stand. As rain began to splash all over the manuscript, notes were vanishing almost as fast, and in some cases faster than I could play them! If some perceptive individual had not photocopied the parts, the performance might well have been *Fair Oak Fusions*' last.

Fortunately, I received the final movement of Rodrigo's *Concierto Como Un Divertimento* at least six months before its first performance, and my work on the Concerto with Joaquin was undoubtedly one of my closest collaborations with a composer.

Opinion has it that there are very few works for cello and orchestra, but this could not be further from the truth. When Rostropovich played his marathon series of concerts in the 1960s nearly forty works were performed — and yet there were still notable omissions. This should have put paid to the myth that there are only a handful of cello concertos but, sadly, only a handful are ever heard. It is the age old vicious circle: as audiences are unfamiliar with lesser known concertos, concert promoters are reluctant to programme them in case their audiences are frightened off. Of all the cello concertos written this century, probably only the Elgar can be said to have become part of the standard repertoire, and even that great masterpiece receives few hearings outside Britain.

What I felt the cello (and cellists) needed was a new concerto which would be popular with audiences and promoters alike. The idea of the composer of the famous *Concierto de Aranjuez* writing a new cello concerto had often appealed to me, but I never thought he would do it. After all, he was nearly eighty, completely blind and had never

117

been a prolific composer.

In the end I have my photographer friend Clive Barda to thank for finally persuading me to write to Rodrigo. Clive has photographed virtually all the world's top musicians and composers and is quite an authority on their whims and peculiarities. One evening, over dinner, we were discussing the whole subject of new cello music and Rodrigo's name was repeatedly mentioned. I voiced my doubts as to whether he would undertake such a large-scale project now, but we agreed there was nothing to be lost by trying.

The next day I wrote my first letter to Rodrigo asking if he would be interested in writing a new Cello Concerto. As I thought he would be interested in Debussy's unusual use of the cello I enclosed my recording of the Debussy and Rachmaninov Sonatas with the letter. After several weeks without reply, the most I expected was a polite but firm refusal. Imagine my surprise when his letter eventually arrived.

'Your musicality and brilliant technique have impressed me. Of course I would like to compose for you a work for cello and orchestra.'

Letters went back and forth and it was finally arranged that I should fly out to meet and play to Rodrigo on my birthday — 14 April. I stayed with Joaquin and his charming wife Victoria for only two days — not nearly long enough to sample the excellence of their Spanish cuisine! During my visit I played Joaquin vast quantities of cello music, sometimes by composers (usually British!) of whom he had never heard.

Nearly all Rodrigo's work has strong Spanish associations, and his music is often inspired by a specific region of Spain (for example, the *Concierto de Aranjuez*). Since Joaquin had already announced he would be dedicating his new concerto to me, I began to wonder, during one rather convivial lunch, whether he might this time consider writing a piece with a British flavour — a sort of *Concierto de Londres*. As I speak no Spanish and Joaquin speaks no English, I directed my question through his wife, and sat back awaiting his reaction.

An incredulous expression slowly dawned on the Maestro's face: '*¡No! ¡No!*' he choked. '*¡Es imposible! ¡Es imposible!*' and I immediately retreated to the safety of a discussion on whether the first movement should have a *tarantella* or *bolero* rhythm.

As might be expected Rodrigo is a strong, determined character. (I soon discovered this when I dared suggest that parts of the new Concerto would be too difficult for many players. 'Es fácil,' he snapped — promptly adding a few more demi-semiquavers). Completely blind since the age of three, he has triumphantly overcome his disability, producing a stream of works which place him firmly in the great Spanish tradition of composers like Albéniz, Turina and Manuel de Falla. His method of working is quite unique. On top of his piano sits a musical Braille machine which he uses to relay the notes on to the manuscript paper. It is an immensely laborious and tiring way of scoring for a full orchestra which makes his achievements all the more remarkable.

Despite the constant carping of some critics, who have found his music 'reactionary', Rodrigo has always remained true to himself, writing exactly what he wants to write. Now eighty-two, he radiates a profound sense of inner peace and I feel honoured to count him among my friends.

In complete contrast to my collaboration with the octogenarian Spaniard, I am now working closely with Peter Skellern on a piece which started life as *Five Love Songs* for cello, piano, vocals and brass (or 'bruss', as Peter would have it). This was premièred at the 1982 Salisbury Festival and the reaction was so favourable that we took it a stage further. Several stages further, in fact, as the project has emerged as a fully-fledged LP called *Oasis*, with Peter, and Mary Hopkin, on vocals and Bill Lovelady and Mitch Dalton on guitars. This was my first recording with the Stradivarius.

So *Travels with my Cello* (my ramble through the byways of music) comes to an end. And the writing of that sentence fills me with both dread and delight. Delight that I have finally managed to finish what at times seemed, in the midst of my journeyings, a positively Herculean task, and dread at the thought of travels *without* my beautiful, if unwieldy, companion — even allowing for all the endless battles with airline officials!

The life of a solo musician is tough and exhausting, both physically and mentally, but I would definitely make the same choice again. For in the end, there is something which sustains you through all the difficulties, something far stronger than ambition, wealth or fame. Let that great cellist, Pablo Casals, say it for me. After a particularly moving performance he was asked:

'Mr Casals, can you tell me, are we in heaven or still on earth?'

Softly, he replied: 'On an earth that is . . . harmonised.'

DISCOGRAPHY

The Voice of the Instrument: J.S. Bach, Bourées from Suite No. 3 in C; Boccherini, Rondo in C; Beethoven, First Movement from Cello Sonata in C, Op., 102, No. 1; Popper, Gavotte No. 2; Saint-Saëns, Allegro Appassionato; Fauré, Elégie; Delius, Cello Sonata; with Clifford Benson, piano. *Discourses – ABK 17*.

Julian Lloyd Webber plays Modern British Cello Music: Fricker, Sonata; Berkeley, Duo; McCabe, Partita; Dalby, Variations (all world première recordings); with John McCabe, piano. *L'Oiseau-Lyre – DSLO 18*.

The Piano Trios of John Ireland: Phantasie Trio, Trio No. 2, Trio No. 3; with Yfrah Neaman, violin and Eric Parkin, piano. *Lyrita – SRCS 98*.

Oration (Concerto Elegiaco) by Frank Bridge (world première recording); with the London Philharmonic Orchestra conducted by Nicholas Braithwaite. *Lyrita – SRCS 104*.

Variations by Andrew Lloyd Webber (world première recording) *MCA – MCF 2824, Cassette TC MCF 2824*.

The Romantic Cello: Popper, Elfin Dance; Saint-Saëns, The Swan; Mendelssohn, Song Without Words; Delius, Romance (world première recording); Saint-Saëns, Allegro Appassionato; Rachmaninov, Slow Movement from Sonata; Elgar, Salut d'Amour; Fauré, Après un Rêve; Chopin, Introduction and Polonaise Brillante; with Yitkin Seow, piano. *ASV – ACM 2002, Cassette ZC ACM 2002*.

Julian Lloyd Webber plays Rachmaninov and Debussy: Rachmaninov, Sonata; Debussy, Sonata; Rachmaninov, Prelude (world première recording), Rachmaninov, Danse Orientale; with Yitkin Seow, piano. ASV – ALH 911, Cassette ZC ALH 911.

Julian Lloyd Webber plays Britten, Ireland and Bridge: Britten, Third Suite for Cello (world première recording); Bridge, Elegy (world première recording); Ireland, Sonata; with John McCabe, piano. ASV – ACA 1001, Cassette ZC ACA 1001.

Fair Oak Fusions by John Dankworth (world première recording). *SEPIA – RSR 1007, Cassette RRT 1007.*

Delius Sonata; with Eric Fenby, piano. *Unicorn-Kanchana – DKP 9021.*

The Fenby Legacy: Delius, Caprice and Elegy; with the Royal Philharmonic Orchestra conducted by Eric Fenby. *Unicorn-Kanchana – DKP 9008/9, Cassette RT 9008/9B.*

Cello Man: Canteloube, Shepherd's Song; Falla, Ritual Fire Dance; Saint-Saëns, Softly Awakes My Heart; Bridge, Scherzetto (world première recording); Fauré, Elégie; Villa-Lobos, Bachianas Brasileiras No. 5; J.S. Bach, Arioso; Popper, Gavotte No. 2; Delius, Serenade from 'Hassan'; Bruch, Kol Nidrei; with the National Philharmonic Orchestra conducted by Charles Gerhardt. *RCA – RL 25383, Cassette RK 25383.*

Julian Lloyd Webber plays Rodrigo and Lalo: Rodrigo, Concierto Como Un Divertimento (world première recording); Lalo, Cello Concerto; with the London Philharmonic Orchestra conducted by Jesús López-Cobos. *RCA – RL 25420, Cassette RK 25420.*

Julian Lloyd Webber plays Delius, Holst and Vaughan Williams: Delius, Cello Concerto; Holst, Invocation (world première recording); Vaughan Williams, Fantasia on Sussex Folk Tunes (world première recording); with the Philharmonia Orchestra conducted by Vernon Handley. *RCA – RS 9010, Cassette RSK 9010.*

Oasis: with Peter Skellern, Mary Hopkin, Bill Lovelady and Mitch Dalton. *WEA-WX3, Cassette WX3C.*

Julian Lloyd Webber plays Haydn Concertos: Concerto in C, Hob. VIIb, No. 1; Concerto in D, Hob. VIIb, No. 4 (world première recording) with the English Chamber Orchestra. *To be released.*

Travels with my Cello: J. Strauss, Pizzicato Polka; Lehar, Vilja (from the Merry Widow); Debussy, Golliwogs Cakewalk; Schumann, Traumerei; Albéniz, Puerta de Tierra; Saint-Saëns, The Swan; Bach/Gounod, Ave Maria; W.S. Lloyd Webber, Andante Affetuoso (world première recording); Rimsky-Korsakov, Flight of the Bumble Bee; Albinoni, Adagio; Trad. arr. Grainger, Londonderry Air; Khatchaturian, Sabre Dance; with the English Chamber Orchestra conducted by Nicholas Cleobury. *Philips 412231–1, Cassette 412231–4, Compact disc 412231–2.*

INDEX

124

125